HOW I CAME TO ACCEPT HIM
LOVING YOUR CHILD FOR WHO THEY ARE

VIVIAN BILLINGS

THE TMG FIRM

New York

The TMG Firm, LLC
112 W. 34th Street
17th and 18th Floors
New York, NY 10120
www.thetmgfirm.com

How I Came To Accept Him: Loving Your Child For Who They Are
Copyright © 2017 Vivian Billings
Published by The TMG Firm, LLC

All rights reserved. No part of this book may be reproduced in any form by any means without the prior written consent of the Publisher. For information address The TMG Firm, 112 W. 34th Street,
17th and 18th Floors,
New York, NY 10120.

For more information about special discounts for bulk purchase, please contact The TMG Firm at 1-888-984-3864 ext 12 or publishing@thetmgfirm.com

ISBN: 978-0-69280-627-2
Library of Congress Control Number: 2017954845

All rights reserved

First The TMG Firm Trade Paperback Edition October 2017
Printed in the United States of America

This is a work of creative nonfiction. The events are portrayed to the best of Vivian Billings' memory. The conversations in this book all come from the author's recollections, though they are not written to represent word-for-word transcripts. Rather, the author has retold them in a way that evokes the feeling and meaning behind what was said and in all instances, the essence of the dialogue is accurate. While all the stories in this book are true, some names and identifying details have been changed to protect the privacy of the people involved.

Cover created by The TMG Firm, LLC.

For Kamal

"This above all:
to thine own self be true..."

-*William Shakespeare*

Hamlet

FOREWORD

They say that being a mother is the hardest job in the world. Despite our accomplishments in life, it's the role of a mother or parent that is the one we are most proud of. So how are we to know that we are doing a good job? What is the measure of success when it comes to your kids? That they grow up? That they go to college? Or that you just outlive them? I'm sure everyone's answer varies.

When Vivian sat across the table from me at Sofrito's in NYC for an episode of *The Gossip Game* and broke down into tears talking about her son's then transition, I immediately connected with her feelings. As the only two mothers on the cast, we had immediately connected because, well, that's what two mothers do when you put them in a situation with five other women who don't have kids. It's that secret moms group that annoys the hell out of those who don't have kids whenever you bring up your kids in a work setting. It's the same feeling that makes you "like" other moms' photos on Instagram whenever they reference their kids or post a silly photo of their kids playing in the snow. It's the "you can't sit with us" type of attitude you take on while raising your kids out of professional insecurity. Viv and I were being featured on a show about being career women in the entertainment industry, but our storylines both included the struggles we were facing with our family at home.

Though I was perceived as the 'OG' on the show, with the most years in the game, Vivian had more experience than I did in one area. She had more and older kids than I did. Therefore, she had more experience as a mother, and I knew I could be facing the same thing she was one day. While health is my main concern when it comes to parenting my kids, my kids' sexuality is something I hadn't even began to think about yet. Vivian was telling me that her daughter wanted to be a man. I didn't know what that felt like.

I had always been so liberal in my views about sexuality. People should be allowed to be who they want to be, I would say. But this was different. How would I feel if my daughter wanted to change her sex? This made me question my position. What if this was my kids' decision?

We talked it through that evening and I hope that I gave Vivian the support she needed in that moment, because I knew I wasn't speaking out of experience. For her, it was only the beginning of what I knew would be a long road. She cried that day on camera, and having not yet done so myself, I knew my tears in front of the world couldn't be held back if I were made to talk about my kids.

Four years have gone by since that dinner, and I still remember how tough it was for Vivian to talk about it so openly. That's why when she called to tell me she was writing a book, I was excited for her. Books are therapy, I always say. It's about coming to terms with something. This is the book I needed to read from Vivian. As a mother of three, I want to know what it feels like, in case I ever had to cross that bridge one day. I always want to be prepared. When it comes to my own journey, if that's a decision one of my kids decides to make, I don't want to be alone. For those who may find themselves in a similar situation as mothers, this book will be the friend you need to consult.

-Kim Osorio

"If you have to choose between doing what you think is 'right' and love, always choose love and you will always be right."

-Susan Cottrell

PREFACE

This book is about my journey of acceptance. In telling my story, you will notice that I will at times refer to Kamal by his birth name and use misgendered pronouns. Though, I understand that both the name and pronouns are not who my son is, or ever was, they reflect where I was in my journey of acceptance at that given time in my life. As my story progresses, you will observe that I no longer use certain pronouns or my son's birth name.

-Viv

PART ONE

Oh God, I thought as my distorted reflection peered back at me from the temporarily clear water at the bottom of the porcelain bowl before me. I was at my best friend Melissa's house hunched over her toilet, in the middle of another wave of nausea. The familiar sensation of my stomach contracting returned and I was once again throwing up what felt like everything I had ever eaten. The experience was far less than pleasing, but I silently thought that it was better than the stomach-wrenching pain from the dry heaving I had experienced earlier in the day. I stared at the vomit in the toilet. As yet another episode of heaving began; my glance shifted to the pregnancy test sitting on the sink. It was positive and the reason why I sat in Melissa's bathroom throwing up everything known to man. I was pregnant again.

Thoughts ran wildly through my head. What was I going to do? I was just 15 years old and pregnant with my second child. How was I going to tell my boyfriend that I was going to have another baby? He did not want to be bothered with our son, Marquis, who was only eight months old at the time. And there I was in the position to have to tell him that I was pregnant again and would be having another child. I did not even want to think about telling him because deep down I already knew exactly what he would say. Plainly stated, he would tell me to end the pregnancy. I pushed the thought of him aside; I did not want to think about his reaction anymore. I did, however, begin to wonder what my parents would think about me being pregnant again. I was worried. I knew they would not approve. They would be mad, hurt and definitely disappointed in me.

Feeling confident that my vomiting had subsided, I hobbled over to the sink to brush my teeth and wash my face. After patting my face dry, I caught a glimpse of myself in the mirror. As I imagined I would, I looked like a train wreck, but I had more important things to worry about than my appearance. I stumbled out of the bathroom and called for Melissa, who had been watching Marquis, while I was preoccupied in the bathroom. Melissa walked over to me with Marquis on her hip. "Well? What does it say?" she asked. I gathered myself and told her the pregnancy test was positive. Needless to say that Melissa was as shocked as I was. If I were not sure of this fact, I was when she screamed, "I don't believe this!" at the top of her lungs.

Melissa, who was generally a good girl, was one of my best friends. To this day, we remain friends, and she was one of the most positive friends I had growing up. We were the total opposite of each other. Nevertheless, I loved her. She was studious, enjoyed school, and she always inspired me to do better. Melissa sincerely asked me what I was going to do about the pregnancy. My response was that I would have an abortion because a second pregnancy felt like too much to bear. Although my mouth spoke of an abortion with ease, I knew it was all talk when the words slid across my lips. Regardless of what I said to Melissa, I knew that I would not dare go through with an abortion; even if it seemed like the right thing to say at the moment.

As I grabbed Marquis from Melissa and placed him on my hip, it was confirmed that my words were not in tune with how I was feeling. I was scared to get an abortion. I never had one, and I did not want to start having any. But I also did not want to deal with disappointing my parents or angering my abusive boyfriend. I did not want to do anything to upset him because I knew that his anger would only serve to stress me out. So in my 15-year-old mind, I decided to do nothing and say nothing. My only recourse was to pray that everything would just disappear. The thought of it had become too much; I was drained. I needed to rest and wanted to go home. So I packed up

Marquis, said goodbye to Melissa, and headed back across the street to my house. As she always would, Melissa watched from her front door as I crossed the street. She never failed to make sure that I was safely in my house before she would go back inside of her own. Just as I was about to cross my front door threshold, Melissa yelled for me to let her know if I needed anything. I sincerely appreciated her concern. I nodded in her direction and entered my house.

Once inside I gave Marquis a bottle and put him down for a nap. As he slept, I laid down on the top bunk in my bedroom and stared at the ceiling. What was I going to do? I was living in my parent's two bedroom apartment, sharing a room with my younger brother and son, and I was pregnant again. I decided to forget all of my concerns and not put off the one call that I knew I had to make. There would never be a right time. I had to call my boyfriend and tell him about the pregnancy. I had to get it over with. I climbed off of the bunk and walked over to the kitchen phone and dialed his number. My stomach twisted itself into knots and turned until it felt as if it had doubled over. It is an understatement to say that I was not looking forward to hearing what he had to say. I hoped he would not answer, but I would have no such luck. Unfortunately, he answered on the third ring. I composed myself and told him that I just found out that I was pregnant. He sighed loudly and immediately started his typical bullshit.

As expected, he was not happy and did not want to hear anything about me being pregnant. He let me know in no uncertain terms that he did not want any more children and that I should have an abortion. I remember wondering if he was so sure that he did not want any other children then why did he continue to have unprotected sex with me? What did he think was going to happen? Besides, what did a second child mean to him? He was acting as if he did anything for Marquis other than complain about him.

I did not want to hear anything else he had to say. I hung the phone up. The best thing for me was to sleep on my decisions. All things considered, I concluded that I would probably feel better after some much-needed rest. I also decided that I no longer wanted to be in a relationship with my boyfriend. When I thought about it, I realized that he was not contributing anything positive to my life. He was not giving me any money. He was not around for our son very often, and he did not do anything for Marquis or me. Granted, his mother would send me a bag of diapers every other week like that meant something, but he did nothing. I was the one stuck with all of the work. I drifted off to sleep with the intention of not stressing myself over his nonsense because I was going to do what I wanted to do anyway.

Months had gone by, four to be exact, and I kept my distance from my boyfriend. I dodged him every chance I got. Although barely noticeable to anyone else, I was beginning to slightly show and I did not want him bothering me because I had made up my mind to keep my baby. No one knew I was pregnant, except for my boyfriend and Melissa. I was keeping my pregnancy a secret; until I could not hide the secret anymore.

I went about life as usual and attended school regularly. One day, after dismissal, while I was preparing to leave a friend of mine informed me that my boyfriend was waiting for me outside. I had no desire to see him. I was doing fine without him so far. I packed up my books and headed for the door, dreading to hear or see what was going to happen next. But my dread did not change the fact that he was outside waiting for me. It was time for me to face the music.

Once out of the door, I rushed right past him as if I did not even see him. He had not called me in almost four months; not even to check on his son. I could not believe that I was pregnant by this fool again. What was I thinking? He ran to catch up with me and asked how I was doing. I told him fine even though I knew what he really wanted to ask. But if he wanted to know, he would have to ask me straight up, and he did. He asked if I had taken care of the last thing I talked to him about. I told him no, and that I was keeping my baby, with emphasis on the *"my baby"* part. I also took the moment to tell him that I did not care if he wanted to stick around or not. I did not want him, and I would take care of both of my children on my own. The words sounded strong as I spoke them, even though I knew they held no real meaning. Despite all that I said, I wanted him to be around. More than anything, I wanted him to step up as a father. But was that ever going to happen? I was not so sure, and I did not have the patience to stick around and find out.

Somehow during our conversation, he convinced me to walk home with him. It was not long before we arrived at his door. When we walked in, he asked me to sit down in the living room and suggested that I get comfortable. I did just that while he asked me if I wanted anything to eat or drink. I told him no. The conversation shifted to my pregnancy and how we could not afford another baby. I openly laughed at his statement because *"we"* had not been doing anything. *"I"* was the one doing all of the work. The remainder of the conversation was not memorable; however, I do remember that I ended up in his bed and we had sex. Admittedly, it felt nice and more than just physically. I felt comfortable and loved; even if only for a brief moment. The feeling was short lived. It ended almost as quickly as it had begun when he rolled over and told me that he would go with me to the Medicaid office the next day to apply for emergency benefits. According to him, we had to go handle the "situation," and we needed to handle it fast.

I knew that there was something more to the polite conversation and intimacy! I knew that he had only brought me to his house for one reason and I was beyond angry. It was all so he could sweet talk me and sleep with me all with the hopes that it would change my mind about the pregnancy. He wanted to paint the picture as if everything would be okay. He wanted to give me the false hope that we would be together as a family. He almost had me convinced. I felt like a damn fool.

Reluctantly, I agreed to go to the Medicaid office with him in an effort to avoid upsetting him. I got up out of his bed, got dressed and left to pick up Marquis from my aunt's house. Of course, I went alone because as per usual my boyfriend did not come with me to pick up our son. He was not involved with us. He never did anything with us. I knew this, and this time it was okay because I needed the time alone to think.

While I traveled to my aunt's house, all of the things my boyfriend said to me earlier replayed in my mind. I wondered if maybe there was a chance that he was right. Maybe I did not need to have the baby. And what exactly was I going to do with another child? I could barely handle Marquis by myself, let alone have another baby. What was I thinking?

The only problem was that I was five months pregnant already. I was confident that my boyfriend did not know how far along I was because he never asked and I did not tell him. I was just in his house, and he did not even know how far along I was in my pregnancy. The sad part was; I knew that he did not care.

Other than my boyfriend, Melissa was the only person who knew of my pregnancy. I had not even gone to the doctors to get checked out. I did not go to any prenatal visits to make sure everything was okay with the baby because I did not know what I was going to do. I just knew I was pregnant because a little stick on my best friend's sink told me that I was. My stomach was getting bigger, and my clothes were fitting me just right. I felt my unborn child move and kick inside of my belly every night. I had no idea how I was going to get through it all. Again the thoughts became too much; therefore, I pushed them aside, picked up Marquis from my aunt's house and headed home.

The next morning I skipped school and met my boyfriend at the bus stop in front of his house. While my family thought I was headed to school, I was actually on my way to the Medicaid office to file for emergency Medicaid along with my good-for -nothing boyfriend. We said nothing to each other the entire bus ride there.

When we arrived, I was surprised to see that there were not as many people there as I thought there would be. Normally, the Medicaid office is filled with all kinds of women, with their babies in tow, looking for some type of assistance. Being as the office was fairly empty, I was seen quickly and approved for Medicaid. Upon my approval, I was informed by my social worker that I needed to have my abortion as soon as possible; within the next six weeks to be exact. The time frame shocked me because by then I was close to being seven months pregnant. I thought to myself, *who does that and how does someone get an abortion that far along?* But I did not verbalize my thoughts. I took my temporary Medicaid card, walked out of the office and told my boyfriend that I was ready to go. Together we left and got on the bus headed away from the Medicaid office. I said nothing the entire ride. This whole scenario was wrong. I also knew entertaining my fool of a boyfriend was wrong too. I led him to believe that I would get the abortion to make him happy. I did not want to fight with him; I just did not have the energy. I did not want the abortion, but I felt like I had no other choice. I desperately wanted my child, but when the thoughts of everything that could go wrong and how difficult my life would be swirled around in my head; I managed to convince myself that maybe an abortion was the best option. I began to think that my boyfriend was right. As soon as we arrived at his house, my boyfriend quickly called the abortion clinic and arranged an appointment for me. It was probably the only thing he ever did for me....besides get me pregnant.

Luckily for him, the abortion clinic told him they had availability for the next morning. They gave him instructions letting me know not to eat anything after midnight and come into the clinic on an empty stomach to have the procedure done. Empty stomach? That was laughable. My stomach was full with a baby. My boyfriend diligently passed along the instructions to me and hung up. He then told me we had to be at the clinic early in the morning and assured me that by the afternoon everything would be all over. Easy for him to say; it was truly just that simple for him. He merely had to take me to the abortion clinic for me to kill my baby, and it would have been over for him. His words stung, but I could not say anything. I looked at him with death in my eyes and decided he was not worth the argument.

I left his house around the time school was to be dismissed to pick Marquis up from my aunt's, considering everyone thought that's where I had been the entire day. I felt terrible and just wanted to be around my son. I wanted nothing more than to hold him in my arms and to reassure him that he was safe with me. I wanted him to feel what I could not at that moment because I did not feel safe at all. I felt like I was trapped in a horrible nightmare. I knew I was not the greatest mom, but I knew I loved my child. And I wanted him to know that. I also knew that despite all that was going on around me; I already loved the baby that I had yet to meet. Ironically, I was preparing for an abortion the very next day. I felt terrible for going along with the decision. I cried all night struggling with the fact that I had resigned myself to getting the abortion. My parents had no idea that I was even pregnant and they never would, considering I was terminating my pregnancy. And all because some damn fool told me I should. In due time I fell asleep, but it was not good sleep at all.

When my alarm rang out at six the next morning, I did not have the energy to climb out of bed. Marquis cried for his bottle, but I could not move. Although unhappy about it, my mother prepared a bottle for him and made sure to come into my room to tell me about it. Without speaking, I rolled my eyes and continued getting ready. I washed up, dressed and got Marquis ready for his return to my aunt's house. Anyone who saw me at the moment would have assumed that the day was just like any other. It was not. In fact, it was far from it. I was going to miss another day of school, and no one knew or cared. It was not possible for my mother to care less. All she seemed to concern herself with was getting drunk and making sure she did not miss work. If I did not interrupt that aspect of her life, she was fine.

I reluctantly met my boyfriend at the same bus stop as I had the day before, but this time we were heading to Manhattan on the E train. With the exception of the background noise that surrounded us, all was pretty quiet the entire trip into Manhattan. When we finally reached our destination, we stood in front of a large industrial building. My boyfriend and I entered the building just as we had any other, headed for the elevator and rode it to the 11th floor. Once the doors parted, we were greeted by a bustling waiting room full of girls and women. They were either completing the necessary forms or waiting to be called to have their "procedure." I was scared shitless, to say the least. As if I were not nervous enough, the office was packed! Just moments before I felt as if I was the only girl in the world in my situation, but as I stood in the middle of the controlled chaos I knew many others were going through the same thing. Still, I had to will myself to move towards the sign-in counter.

Without the faintest of smiles or a greeting of any type, the nurse behind the counter handed me the forms to fill out. As she slid the papers towards me, she plainly said, "Please sign your name if you haven't already done so and fill out these forms." The atmosphere was dark, and there was a gloom that hung over the room. I truly did not want to be there, but I took the forms then found a seat in the waiting room. My boyfriend was on my heels attempting to find out the type of information the forms required, but I was in no mood to share anything with him. He was the reason I was there in the first place. Anger began to well inside of me because I did not want to be there. As I stared around the room, I noticed that everyone else seemed to be acting as if this was just another day in the life for them. I wondered if I was the only person in there who was not okay with getting an abortion. Or at the very least did any of the others share my doubts? And I had many. One of which was, why was I there? Was it because I worried about getting my ass whipped by my boyfriend for not following his directions? I was not sure, and as the weight of the question began to bear down on me, I started to get dizzy. My solution was to distract myself by completing my paperwork. The entire time I worked on my forms and even after I returned them to the unfriendly nurse, my boyfriend sat quietly. He did not make the slightest of sounds or utter one word to me. Although he had so much to say to me the day before, on this day he was mute. I wondered why, even though I was pretty sure of the answer. Either way, regardless of his reasoning, I was without question done with him after my "procedure."

We sat in the waiting room for about a half hour before a nurse called me. At the sound of my name, everything began to move in slow motion. I looked up at the nurse and all of the others in the waiting room. I was met by all of their gazes. Then almost unbelievably, I heard a whisper in my ear saying, "Don't do this. This isn't right." A lump formed in my throat as the nurse called my name for the second time. As tears formed in my eyes, I stood from the chair as if I were going to follow the nurse, but my feet quickly took me in the opposite direction towards the elevators. I could not do it. I was not going to do it; not that day, not the day after, not ever!

I made the decision right then and there to pick up my son from my aunt's house and go home to tell my parents that I had, yet again, messed up. I did not know what the consequences would be and quite frankly I did not care. I was going to keep my baby regardless. That's just the way it was going to be. I also did not give a second thought to how my boyfriend felt; who was, by the way, right behind me at that point.

I honestly thought that he was going to be angry with me, but to my surprise, he was not. He did, however, plead with me to return to the clinic to continue with the "procedure." He begged and begged. He even feigned sincerity and put on the sweetest act he could muster in an effort to convince me to go back, but it was too late. I was done! So I pretended I did not hear him and kept walking as if he did not even exist. My eyes were set on the train station as I jogged away from the abortion clinic. I wanted no parts of that place; never had and never will!

My boyfriend huffed, puffed and sighed as he attempted to maintain my pace. I could tell that he wanted to continue his point for the abortion, but I did not care what he had to say or any consequence that I was going to face. I could not care less about anyone talking about me and pointing out that I was sixteen pregnant with my second child. I simply did not care. My mind was made up. I had accepted the fact that I was going to have another child. I just was not so sure how I was going to break the news to my parents. So, for the time being, I decided to continue to keep my pregnancy a secret. As fate would have it, I later learned that my parents had grown tired of living in our cramped apartment and had recently been approved to purchase a house they were interested in buying. They wanted to move out of Queens as soon as possible, and the approval came at the perfect time. We were heading to Long Island. It was a long way from Queens, that's for sure. I could not wait to leave. I wanted to get the hell out of there and away from the madness; even if it was madness that I had created for myself. But the move would come later.

Later that day, I got off of the train and made the trip home alone after my boyfriend realized that I was not changing my mind about the baby. As an adult, I recognize that it was something he often did. He had no problem letting me do things on my own. I can now clearly see how he was never there for my kids or me, but for some strange reason, I stayed with him. I have no idea why and have yet to find an answer as to why I stayed with him for so long. Outside of my children, who I love very much, I can't seem to figure out why I wasted so much time with a person who did not care about me.

I ended up not telling my parents that I was pregnant, or that I had missed school for the last two days. I acted as if everything was normal. I did, nonetheless, decide to schedule a doctor's appointment to make certain the baby and I were okay. I rationalized that I had that emergency Medicaid and there was no better use than prenatal care.

I made an appointment in August to have my first prenatal visit. I was six months pregnant, and Marquis had just turned a year old. I had not had any prenatal care, including taking the vitamins, and had basically winged it for the first six months of my pregnancy. At my first appointment, I found out that I was going to have a girl. I was so excited. I wanted a daughter since I already had my son.

In keeping with his m.o., my boyfriend never came with me to any of my doctor's appointments because he was mad that I decided to continue the pregnancy. I gave him ample opportunities to join me, but he never did. Oddly enough I was okay with him not joining me because I would soon be moving and getting away from him.

My parents still did not know I was pregnant, but I promised myself that I would tell them soon. Although I was pleased to be able to tell them about my pregnancy in my own time, I found it odd they never noticed my weight gain or that my stomach had begun to poke out. Either they did not notice and were oblivious, or they did not care. Admittedly I took full advantage that baggy clothes were in style. For me the baggier the clothes, the better; to the outside world I looked fashionable, not pregnant.

August 31st, moving day, came fast. My family and I packed up our moving truck and headed to our new home in Long Island. In all of my young life, I had never seen my dad so excited. Before moving day arrived, he would drive Marquis, my younger brother and me past our new house and tell us we would be living there soon. He was extremely proud of his purchase and loved sharing with us all of the wonderful things about where we would be staying. And just as he had said, it was great. I loved the new house. Marquis had his own room, and I had my own room and bathroom. In fact, I had the entire upstairs to myself. It felt as if I had my own apartment. The accomplishment of purchasing his first home was one of my dad's proudest moments; especially since he did not have the most reputable past. My dad also had a child when he was fifteen. I guess it can be said that I was following the footprints of his past.

I felt bad about not being able to tell my dad about my pregnancy because I wanted to tell him. I knew, without a doubt, that he would take the news a lot better than my mom. He was cool like that. Experience had shown me that he would initially be mad, but would soon be over it. My mom was a different story altogether. She would bring up things that happened in the 70's like it happened the day before and I just could not deal with her. She had many addictions when I was growing up, and because of that, I found myself in a lot of situations I should have never been in. I did not like my mom; at all. She could have been the last person on Earth, and I would not want to talk to her; let alone tell her my personal business.

My dad was so happy about the new house and the new school my brother and I would be attending that I did not want to ruin it. So instead of telling him about my pregnancy, I remained quiet. Luckily, the summer came and went by smoothly without anyone discovering my secret.

The first day of school rolled around, and after a brief conference with the guidance counselor, I received my class schedule for the new year. I looked at my schedule and could not believe my luck. Gym was my first class of the day. There was no way I could participate in gym first thing in the morning. I wasted no time and headed straight to the gymnasium. I notified my teacher that I was pregnant and could not participate in any of the class activities. She responded that I needed a note from my doctor stating that I was pregnant and dismissing me from activities. I told her that I would bring a note, but I knew that I had one small problem. I was new to the area and had not had the opportunity to find a doctor in Long Island. Although I knew it would take some time, I was determined to find me a doctor so I could be excused from attending gym class.

Weeks passed by without me getting a doctor's note as my gym teacher requested. I began to get a little nervous because I had not found a doctor and my teacher continued to ask for my excuse note. I can only assume that she grew tired of waiting and called my parents to find out what was going on because when the weekend came, I was in for a big surprise.

On this particular weekend, I had gone back to Queens with Marquis to visit my boyfriend. It was something I would occasionally do so that he could see his son. My boyfriend never seemed too interested, but I was nonetheless excited to leave Long Island because I thought it was boring. I could not wait to go back to Queens and be around my real friends. I left school that Friday afternoon, picked Marquis up from the sitter, and went home to pack our clothes. Once I was done, I headed for the LIRR (Long Island Rail Road). I got on that train with Marquis thinking that it would be a weekend filled with relaxation and visits with friends. Boy was I wrong!

When I got off of the train and made the long walk from Sutphin Boulevard to Atlantic Avenue, I felt something weird. Maybe it was a vibe or something of the sort, but I did not like what I was feeling. I could not place exactly what it was, but I found out as soon as I neared my boyfriend's house. I looked up to see my parent's car parked in front of his house and I could not figure out why. Maybe they were there to meet with my boyfriend's mother in an attempt to get him more involved with Marquis. My parents knew that he did nothing for his son and they were sick of him. My father especially did not like my boyfriend at all. If he had it his way, my boyfriend would have been dead somewhere. But for some reason, I did not think my parents were at my boyfriend's house on Marquis's behalf. I can't tell you why, but I felt they were there for something else. Whatever their reason, I was going to have to face it head on.

I opened the door to my boyfriend's house with Marquis in tow to find everyone sitting in the living room. I greeted them all as if I had not a care in the world. Marquis ran over to my dad, gave him a high five and sat next to him.

When I looked around the room, I could see my parents were not happy, and neither was my boyfriend's mother. She was the first one to respond to my greeting in her thick Jamaican accent. She then walked over to me and without a care for who was in her home, lifted my shirt in front of everyone. I tried to suck in my stomach as fast as I could, but it was no use. My exposed belly, full of stretch marks, popped out. The jig was up. Everyone knew I was pregnant.

My boyfriend's mother asked, "Vivian, are you pregnant again?" I did not reply.

My mother said, "She can't be pregnant! Pregnant where? I would've noticed if my daughter was pregnant."

I inhaled deeply. *Tuh!* Who was my mother trying to fool?

My boyfriend's mother spoke again. "Vivian, are you really seven months pregnant?" I did not answer. Tears started to form in my eyes. I could not hold them back any longer, and I began to cry in front of everyone. They all somehow knew that I was pregnant. But how? I wondered who could have told them?

My father's voice broke me from my thoughts as he demanded that I tell them what was going on. My mother chimed in and told me that my gym teacher had called inquiring about a doctor's note explaining that I was pregnant and could not participate in gym. She went on to say that my teacher informed them that she had been asking for the note for weeks. I could not keep my secret any longer; there was no use in trying. I shook my head and confirmed to everyone in the room that I was indeed pregnant. My mother's response was that there was nothing that could be done because I was too far along to get an abortion. She had no idea about what had occurred at the abortion clinic a few months before. She would have loved for me to have aborted my baby, but I did not let that happen. Even with all of the confusing emotions going through my head, I felt a weight had been lifted off of my shoulders. I felt free. I did not have to hide anymore. I did not have to feel like I had to keep a secret that would unquestionably come to light. I felt relieved.

Although he was disappointed, I knew my Dad would come around in the end. I had every faith that he would help me out with the baby, just as he had always helped me out. My dad was someone I could always count on. He was the best. He was reliable, and he loved Marquis. I was sure he would love my new baby just the same. He would just need a few days to get over the shock of everything that had just taken place, but he would turn around. He always did.

PART TWO

Just a few weeks after the news broke of my second pregnancy, I had an appointment at the local clinic and began visiting my doctor regularly. Under my doctor's care, I began taking prenatal vitamins and iron pills. My doctor also told me to relax and take it easy for the remainder of my pregnancy.

Around December 22nd I received a call from Southside Hospital, in Bay Shore, N.Y., informing me that if I did not deliver my baby by December 29th, they would have to schedule me for a C-section. To say I was shocked is a gross understatement. Did they know who I was? Did they not know that Vivian did not do well with needles of any kind, let alone surgery? To avoid the possibility of surgery, I went right into my medicine cabinet and drank me a substantial amount of castor oil. I woke up in the middle of the night on December 24th with stomach cramps. The cramps were not severe. They felt almost as if I had to have a bowel movement. The pain was bearable, and I assumed that it had everything to do with the tacos I devoured the night before. It never occurred to me that the castor oil may have played a factor in the cramps I was experiencing in the middle of the night.

Thinking that it was the tacos, I got up from bed to take a relaxing shower; after which I tried to go back to sleep. The only problem was that the pain grew worse; so much so that I could not go to sleep at all. I was up all night with cramps.

Around 9 am the next morning, I went downstairs to let my parents know that I was not feeling well and I thought that I should go to the hospital. My mother was not too thrilled because my going to the hospital interfered with her plans to go out for the day. She would now have to stay home and watch Marquis while my father took me to the hospital to be examined. I was in so much pain that my mother's attitude was the least of my concerns. I told her I needed to go to the hospital and I needed to go right then. I suppose the urgency in my voice made her realize that I was serious and she reluctantly told my father to take me to the hospital.

My father carefully helped me into his car and off to the hospital we went. He was extremely nervous and constantly checked on me the entire ride. Shortly after I was checked into the maternity ward, I was connected to the monitor and sure enough, I was indeed having contractions. However, I was only dilated about two centimeters, so they suggested I walk up and down the hallways of the hospital to encourage further dilation. My father was a good sport and waited patiently in the waiting room. As I continued my walk through the hallways, I stopped by to see my dad. He expressed his concern that I had somehow managed to walk all the way from the maternity ward to the waiting room. I assured him I was doing as I was told. Hey, they told me to walk right? Although I was in a building full of people trained to help me in any way that I needed, my father sincerely and considerately reassured me that he would be right there in the waiting room. He then told me to let him know if I needed anything from him.

Considering the amount of pain that I was in, I was not sure if I would need anything from him unless he had some pain killers in his pockets. But I just nodded appreciatively and then headed back to the maternity ward. As I walked away, the pain became unbearable, and my knees buckled. At the sight of this, my Dad grew increasingly worried and thought it was best to follow me back to the maternity ward to ensure I was okay. I hobbled along the hallways until I reached the nurse's station, where I told them I could not walk any longer. This was enough for them to finally put me into a room. I heard later that they allowed my father to come up from the main waiting room to the one in the maternity ward, which was just a few feet away from my room.

I was in my room for only a brief period before the nursing staff informed me that it was time for me to deliver the baby. I was in incredible pain and did not want to be alone while I delivered, so I asked them to get my father. I was not prepared when one of the nurses informed me that my father was no longer in the waiting room. The information rested on my lap like a ton of bricks. *What? Where the hell did he go? He was just there not too long ago!* I wanted and needed answers, but my body told me that any answer I was expecting would have to wait. It was time for me to deliver my baby; it was pushing time. The entire time I was pushing, I was exactly where I did not want to be; by myself. Oh, how I wished someone could have been with me, if for no other reason than to just stand beside me. But that was just not the case. I ended up telling myself that being alone was my punishment for keeping my pregnancy a secret the entire time.

At 1:50 pm on Christmas Eve of 1993, Kadijah Shontelle Thompson was born. She weighed 6 pounds 5 ounces and was 19 inches long. I remember the doctor asking me if I wanted to hold her and I did for a little while. She felt so tiny in my arms compared to Marquis, who was almost 8 pounds at birth. The joy I felt holding her was only matched by how tired I suddenly felt. Out of nowhere, I was extremely tired. I suspect it was because I did not have an epidural during delivery. I had my Kadijah au naturel and felt as if I had worked out in the gym for hours. I asked the nurse to please take my baby girl from me because I needed to sleep. I was damn near falling asleep with her in my arms, and that was a definite no-no. Because there weren't any rooms available at the time, I ended up falling asleep on the delivery table with my baby girl next to me. The table was comfortable enough, and my body had tapped out.

I was awakened about an hour later by a transport nurse after a room had finally become available. For a moment, I almost forgot where I was because the delivery room was so peaceful and quiet. I looked over at my baby girl only to discover that she was no longer there. The transport nurse informed me that they had taken her to be cleaned up and reassured me that she would meet me in my room. That's when I remembered to ask about my dad again and was told that he had left a long time ago. *Really?*

How could he just leave me like that? I had my baby girl all by myself. I was alone. My baby's father did not bother to witness her birth. I cried as I was transported through the hospital all alone. I had just turned 16 years old two months earlier and thought this would be a special day for my family. I was sadly mistaken.

Once I arrived to my room, the transport nurse helped me get situated, including informing me that I had access to a phone and television. She made sure I was comfortable before leaving and asked if I needed anything. I did not, and told her as such; however, as soon as she left the room I reached for the phone to call my house to see what was going on. My priority was to make sure that my dad was okay. My mom picked up the phone and in her typically nasty tone asked me if my father had to drive back to the hospital to pick me up. I pulled the phone away from my ear and stared at it for a second. I could not understand her response or why she was so angry. In a tone, just as nasty as hers, I shot back, "No! I had my baby!" The information caught her off guard, and I knew it when, "What?" was her only response.

My mom quickly changed her tune. She said the hospital staff told my dad to go home because I probably would not deliver until later in the evening. They also told him that they would call him back when I was ready. I was mortified! *How could they do that, especially when I asked for him during my delivery?* Nevertheless, my father was okay, and my mind was at ease. He came to the phone and told me that he would pick me up once I was discharged. I was okay with that and said goodbye. Not long after that call, the hospital staff brought my beautiful daughter in for me to bond with and make an attempt to breastfeed. After several unsuccessful tries, I asked for formula. I was tired, and my baby was hungry.

With the exception of my paternal grandmother, who brought my mother along, no one visited me my entire three day stay in the hospital; and they were only there for about 20 minutes. My boyfriend and father of my children was nowhere to be found, and he made no attempt to visit me either. My parents called him and told him that I had the baby. Alas, since he lived in Queens, he was in no rush to make it out to see the baby and me. Although on the day I was discharged from the hospital, he did come over to my parent's house, along with his younger brother, to watch Marquis for my mother. I'm sure that made her happy since she hated watching kids.

When the time came for me to be discharged, I could not wait to leave the hospital. I was ready and felt as if my baby was ready as well. I had everything we needed packed and prepared to go. It was freezing cold outside. For our travels home, I had my baby girl dressed in a furry, pink all-in-one coat and a hat with a bow on it. Thankfully my dad had purchased a car seat because he knew my boyfriend would not get one. When I arrived home, I was not happy to see my boyfriend or his brother. To me, his presence meant more work. In addition to me watching Marquis and my newborn baby, I knew that I would end up having to clean up after them. That moment solidified for me that I would rather take care of two babies by myself before I would be bothered with his no good ass.

My boyfriend did not stay long, and as expected he did not help out with Kadijah. I felt nothing but relief when he and his brother left my parent's house two days later, I was relieved. When he finally left, I did not call him, nor did I go and visit him. I was enjoying my daughter, who was, by the way, an extremely good baby. She was not cranky in the least. She woke up every four hours like clockwork for a bottle and looked a lot like Marquis. The two of them were instantly inseparable. I found it adorable that Marquis wanted to know who this extra little person was taking up his mommy's time.

As they grew older, I noticed that my daughter did not like playing with dolls. She wanted to play with trucks and Power Rangers just like Marquis. I was intermittently involved with their father, who had since moved to Long Island to be closer to me; or at least that is what his mother said. Even with his move to Long Island, we did not see each other as often as one would expect. It was as if he still lived in Queens. The move did not prompt him to spend more time with his kids either, so it was back to the same old crap! But one day, out of the blue, he had asked the kids and me to take a ride with him to Brooklyn to visit his family. Along the way, he made a pit stop at his cousin's house. I was not doing anything that day, so I thought a family ride together would be nice for the kids and me.

The ride to Brooklyn went fairly smoothly and without incident. Everything seemed to be going well. When we arrived at his cousin's, I decided to wait in the car with the kids because I did not feel like going inside. It was not long before I found out why we made the stop at his cousin's. My boyfriend made the stop to pick up two pounds of weed from her boyfriend. I was furious. I could not believe that he had my children and I involved in his bull! How could that asshole pretend that we were taking a leisurely ride to visit family, only to turn around and jeopardize my family?! I wanted to get the hell out of there and fast. I was just about to jump out of the car with my kids when out of nowhere an unknown female jumps into the back seat of the car with my two children. I turned around and said, "Who the hell are you?" She replied with a name, but to this day I can't tell you what it was because my ears were filled with heat and all I saw was red!

Not too long after the unknown woman got into the car, my boyfriend joined us as if it was normal to ride around with strangers. He started the car without so much as offering an explanation as to who the woman was. And when I asked him, his response was for me to "stop bugging him" because he was just taking her to the train station as a favor to his cousin. It was only a 10-minute ride to the train station, and neither the stranger or my boyfriend said a word to each other before we dropped her off. When she exited the car, I could no longer contain my anger. I exploded and told him exactly what I thought of him. I screamed at the top of my lungs all while telling him he was putting our family, my family, in danger. We were on the Southern State Parkway, and I was going crazy. Any obscenity that can be thought of was coming out of my mouth. Marquis, who was six at the time, and Kadijah, who was five, were in the back seat of the car frozen, shocked and clueless to what the argument was actually about.

In the midst of my yelling, my boyfriend slapped me. It was not the first time he had done so, but it would be the first time I punched him back in front of the kids. He grabbed a handful of my long hair and continuously bashed my head into the dashboard. It was the middle of the night, and we were swerving across the highway as we fought. My children were so upset with their father that they leaned across the front seat and grabbed his arm. They repeatedly pleaded with him saying, "Let go of Mommy!" I remember everything stopping right before he turned around and pushed the kids down into the back seat. He then told them if they ever touched him again, he would kill them! I was hysterical, but I knew I would never allow him to hurt my children. I would die before I let anything happen to them!

The bastard finally let me go. He screamed at the top of his lungs that if the cops were out and decided to pull us over, we would have gone to jail and lost our kids. His dumbass had no idea that was exactly what I was thinking when we were in Brooklyn parked in front of his cousin's house. I stayed quiet, grabbed the side of my head which was by then aching in pain. I calmed the children down the best I could and sat numbly, while tears streamed down my cheeks for the rest of the ride. My head hurt terribly. Judging by the locks of hair all over the floor, I knew precisely why my head was hurting. My forehead was covered in knots from being bashed into the dashboard, and my children were horrified. I could no longer live like that; I had to do better.

When he pulled in front of my house and stopped the car, he warned me not to think about breaking up with him and said he would come the next day to check on me. I did not say anything. I could not look at him. I got out of the car slowly with my children and went into my house. My parents were in the living room when I walked in. My dad was the first one to get up off the couch to ask me what happened. I told him everything, and he promptly told me the father of my children, whose name I refuse to mention because of his insignificance in my life, was no longer welcomed in the house. The next thing he did was call his brother Noel, who was known for giving respectable advice.

I could hear my Uncle Noel telling my dad, who rightfully wanted nothing more than to kill the father of my children, to calm down. My dad passed me the phone, and I spoke to my uncle who advised me to call the cops and file a report. I was not cool with calling the cops, but my uncle reassured me that it was the best thing to do in my current situation because it created a paper trail in the event that the father of my children tried to harm my kids. Uncle Noel also told me that I should get an order of protection against him, so he would not be able to come near us. And that is exactly what I did.

The cops came to my house that night. I filed a report as my uncle had suggested, but I did not want to file any charges. I also got an order of protection against the father of my children so that he could not come near us again. Additionally, I also went to court to file for child support since he had never given me any money in the first place. Would you believe he did not even want to help support his flesh and blood? It would take him years, several arrests and violations of court orders, coupled with $65,000 in arrears for him to even consider paying me any support. But my nightmare with him was over. Thankfully, I would never again have to worry about him laying a finger on me ever again.

PART THREE

After the unspeakably horrendous day on the Southern State Parkway, it was just my children and me. We were by ourselves; with the exception of my dad, who helped a lot, and my grandmother, who helped out when she could. My children, especially my daughter, watched as I went through other relationships that did not work out. I assume it was those failed relationships and the fact that her father was never around, that made her not care for men so much. She was always standoffish and seemed to have a perpetual attitude. She was a tough one to raise, particularly since I was raising two children on my own.

Occasionally, my dad would take my children along with some of the neighborhood children, to Great Adventures while I was at work. He was just that kind of man. He loved kids, and he loved me. He helped out so much that Marquis wanted to start calling him Dad instead of Grandpa.

Meanwhile, Kadijah was constantly cutting up in school. She was always fighting or talking back to the teachers. This lead me to decide to get my children counseling. I figured they might have needed it, considering their dad was rarely around. I thought it would be therapeutic for them to discuss what was on their mind in a judgment free atmosphere with the hopes they would gain relief from whatever may have been troubling them.

Pretty soon things started to turn around for my children and me. I had finally met a great guy, who my children liked. My dad loved him, and things were going well. The new guy in my life took me on trips and helped me pay for my children's daycare. He helped me out in any way he could, including showing that he loved my children and me. After much heartache in my earlier life, I had found the one. I would go on to marry him and we would have three children together. Life was going great. That is until, November 03, 2002, when my father tragically died in a horrific car accident. It caught us all by surprise. We were all in utter shock and disbelief. When I received that fateful call, the hospital did not tell me exactly what happened. They simply told me to come to the hospital because my father had been in a car accident. I had no idea what I was in for, but when I arrived at the hospital, they told me my father had passed away. I could not think straight. I had just spoken to him the night before. Everything moved in slow motion for me. My father, my rock, who had supported me through everything, was gone and he was not coming back. It hit me like a ton of bricks, and I felt as if I could not breathe.

My entire family was devastated by my father's passing. My mother, who by my estimation was already screwed in the head, became even worse. It was as if she could no longer function. To this day, my mom has not recovered from my father's passing. Marquis, who was not one to often cry, broke down in tears when he leaned over my father's casket at the funeral home. He was only ten years old, and my heart broke at the outward expression of his pain. My children's main father figure and true positive male influence had been taken from their lives. We were left to figure out life without him by our sides. It was, without question, the worst thing that ever happened to us. And I had been through a lot.

My father's death took an incredibly big toll on my children. Marquis's grades slipped, and he began to barely get by in school. Regardless of what I took from him as a form of punishment, he no longer cared enough about school. It was as if nothing held any importance after my father passed away.

Kadijah's fights occurred more and more frequently. The level of disrespect she held for generally everything became intolerable. It was to the point that I began to ask myself if the pain was ever going to stop. My husband tried to help in any way he could, but it just was not the same without my father. Besides, I did not want to burden my husband with all of my problems.

After the death of my dad, I started to see a change in Kadijah. I could not quite put my hands on what the change was, but there were signs of what was to come. I pushed them to the back of my mind as my family dealt with the aftermath of losing my dad. If asked, I would say that the first sign was Kadijah's choice of friends. She had one particular friend named Paris who she would always hang around. The two were inseparable. Kadijah was about 14 years old when Paris began coming around the house. I noticed there was something different about Paris. She was not the stereotypical girlie girl, but I did not give it much thought and thanked God that she was not one of the promiscuous little girls in the neighborhood.

On Marquis' birthday, he wanted to celebrate it with friends at Great Adventures. I thought it sounded like a fun idea. I planned it out and called every invited friend's parent. Kadijah begged me to let Paris accompany us because she did not want to go anywhere without her. I agreed. We had a marvelous day together. Looking back on the ride to Great Adventures, I distinctly remember Kadijah and Paris in the third row of my SUV. They were laughing and giggling as if they were sharing their own little secrets. When I looked in my rear view mirror, I could not see anything that they were possibly doing wrong, but it seemed that something just was not right between them. *What in the hell were they up to?*

Outside of the ride to the amusement park, I recall Kadijah telling me about an argument she once had with Paris. From my vantage point, the argument was similar to one between a dating couple. However, my daughter knew I did not allow boyfriends and girlfriends; especially at the age of 14. So I accepted the story as a typical argument between friends. But then one day, just like that, Paris disappeared. It was as if she never existed. I asked Kadijah what happened between the two of them. She blew me off with a simple, "Nothing." That was enough for me to assume they had simply stopped being friends. *Eh! Oh well. Later Paris!*

Suddenly and out of the blue, Kadijah began to ask me to buy her new clothes. Normally, the clothes I purchased fit her well. Sometimes they were slightly bigger, but that was only because she had a big behind for a young girl. Just the same, I took notice when she started asking for clothes that were double her size. I chose not to say anything because at one point, during the early 90's, I wore baggy clothes as well. So I never mentioned it, but made a mental note to myself. I passed it off as a phase and figured that she would grow out of liking that particular style; just as I had years earlier. It was all a phase, or at least that is what I convinced myself to believe.

Time went on, and things started to get better. I once again had my children in counseling to deal with the pain of losing their grandfather. The counseling helped, and soon we were able to adjust to my father's absence. And that's when it happened.

I was in the kitchen at my mother's house with my grandmother, and we were talking about a friend of mine, Linda, who had recently found out that her daughter was gay. Linda was mortified because she did not hear the news from her daughter, but rather heard it from her daughter's girlfriend's parents. The news was mind blowing and embarrassing for Linda because she had no clue that her daughter was gay, nor had she seen see any signs. As I told my grandmother the story, Kadijah walked into the kitchen and attentively listened as we spoke. She did not say anything at first, she just listened. It was not until she heard me say that I would never be mad at my children for being gay, and I would only be upset if I had to find out through the streets rather than them telling me directly. That's when Kadijah spoke up. "Really?" she asked. To which I replied, "Yeah! Who wants to hear about their child from the streets?" Kadijah then openly admitted to both my grandmother and me that she was a lesbian.

I looked at Kadijah without a trace of surprise and told her I already knew. She looked at me and was astonished at my response. I smiled and thanked her for being honest, and she went about her business. My grandmother did not say a word.

She only smiled. I asked her if the news bothered her, and she said, "No, Kadijah's always been a little funny." We both laughed, and that was the end of it.

From that day, Kadijah became very comfortable with her newfound sexuality. She was only 15 years old, and now that she knew I was okay with her being a lesbian, she began to bring girls home. I did not care if she was gay or straight; she would not disrespect my household. That's what she was not going to do!

It did not take long before Kadijah started bringing a girl named Latonya over to the house. In all honesty, I truly disliked Latonya. She was a pretty girl and all, but she was about 17 or 18 years old; which was entirely too old for Kadijah. From what I remember about Latonya was that she had tattoos all over her neck, chest area, arms, and hands. She even had piercings...Lord the piercings! I am not inherently against tattoos and piercings because I have my fair share of both. But this was a young girl, and it gave me the indication that her parents may not have been too involved in her life;

which meant they probably did not care about her either. *Just my luck!*

I soon found out that Latonya was indeed going to be a problem for me. Her parents allowed her to do as she pleased, while Kadijah had her fair share of restrictions. Latonya was allowed to stay out late and drive her mother's car wherever she wanted, whenever she wanted. She was clearly allowed to get tattoos and piercings, where Kadijah was not. It was in this detail where my problem lied. Kadijah started to hate me because of the restrictions placed on her and soon became defiant. She would sometimes leave late at night and not return, without so much as a phone call to let me know as to where she was. When she decided to tell me where she was going, she would not come home on time. She would steal money from me to hang with Latonya while I was at work. Kadijah would also steal money from her little sister's piggy banks. It hurt me more than imaginable when she stole my diamond earrings to go out and look cool with Latonya at the Manhattan PRIDE parade. Those earrings were a gift from my husband and were one of the first presents that I ever received from a man outside of my father. They were beyond special to me and held an irreplaceable sentimental value to me.

I began to feel that I had no control when it came to Kadijah. She would curse at me when I tried to talk to her, and our arguments grew increasingly worse. My child was not listening to me, and I had three other children besides her to take care of. I felt helpless, and the cycle of bullshit went on for months!

One day Kadijah did not come home. However, I knew exactly where she was. She was at Latonya's house. I staked out Latonya's house with the hopes of catching Kadijah to teach her a lesson. I had grown to hate Latonya, and I hated her mother even more. Kadijah, on the other hand, loved them. *Who had my daughter become?* I started to feel like I did not know her anymore. I ended up calling the police to come to Latonya's house to make Kadijah leave. I was desperate. I wanted my daughter out of that house and back home where she belonged.

The police came, barged into Latonya's mother's house and searched for Kadijah. Latonya's mother came out of the house cursing. She also told me that I had no control over my daughter and it was not her fault that I could not keep my child under control. Her words stung. It bothered me that she said them, but she had a valid point. I had no control over my child, and it was time I started having some.

Unfortunately for me, Kadijah was not at Latonya's when the police arrived. I'm certain she left through the back door and headed home when she realized I was not playing with her anymore. When I returned home after the entire ordeal, Kadijah was home on the computer as if nothing had happened. I instructed Marquis to take his little sister upstairs while I handled matters with Kadijah. I was at my breaking point. Needless to say, tempers flared, and things got out of control.

The next day she went to school, and as one would expect, CPS soon paid a visit to my house. With the latest turn of events, Kadijah thought she had it all in the bag. Little did she know that I was ready to sign over my parental rights to the state of New York. Despite my intentions, the state was not inclined to consent. *Oh no, sir!* New York State wanted you to keep your bad ass, out of control children until they were the tender age of 21!

As it turned out, I ended up building a great relationship with my CPS worker, and he informed me that I could get Kadijah arrested for her erratic and out of control behavior. This was like music to my ears. I never wanted to be the parent who sent their child to jail, but Kadijah left me no other choice. It was to the point where I was scared to leave her younger siblings alone with her. My home had ceased to be the peaceful respite it once was. I had to lock my money and jewelry in the safe anytime I left the house. And my mother installed a lock on her bedroom door out of fear that something of importance would go missing. We couldn't trust Kadijah to save our lives, and we lived under those conditions for months! Therefore, whenever she started her nonsense, I would call 911. It was disheartening to find out that the police could not arrest her because, at the age of 15 years old, she was considered a minor. *Damn!*

There I was attempting to show my child tough love, and it was not working. After I called the police on her a few more times, Kadijah began to fear that she would be arrested at some point and her behavior soon improved. As a result, I elected to have a surgery that I needed and asked Kadijah to help me out with her siblings while I was temporarily out of commission. It was a mistake that I would soon regret.

I was in so much pain after my surgery that I asked Kadijah to come straight home after school to help me with the children. She came, but she was not alone; she brought the last person I wanted to see, Latonya. We started arguing because I did not want Latonya in my house after the earlier incident at her house. Things became even uglier between Kadijah and I. So much so that she ended up punching me in my stomach directly where I recently had surgery. I felt a jolt of excruciating pain and could not believe what had happened. I was hurt literally and figuratively. The blow almost took me down to the floor. I was furious.

My child had punched me while I was in pain, and vulnerable from surgery. To make matters worse, she did it in front of Latonya. I used what strength I had to run to the kitchen and grabbed the biggest kitchen knife I could find. I then chased Kadijah and Latonya out of my house. Marquis came out of his room to find out what the commotion was and to make sure that I was okay. He was as shocked as I was. He could not believe his sister was acting out in that way. My younger daughters were scared to death of their older sister, and I no longer wanted her in my house.

After Kadijah and Latonya were gone, I went into her room and packed all of her things. I left all of it on the front steps. There was no way she was coming back into the house. I even changed the locks to make sure she could not just walk back in. I called her father and told him, point blank, that Kadijah could no longer live with me. It was time for him to step up and be a father. I let him know that all of her belongings were on the front steps and directed him to come get her. I could not believe it when he wanted to know if I was going to lower his child support payments since he would be taking her. He had some damn nerve. He had never done anything for my children, but the minute he thought he was helping me out, he wanted to lower the child support. I told him that I would lower his payments, but in the back of my mind, I knew better. I was not doing anything for him.

He did not have Kadijah for a week before he turned up at my door with Kadijah and her belongings. He said she could not stay at his house any longer because she was too out of control. *Huh? It must have been nice.* Kadijah was at her father's house for a whopping five days, and during that time, she got a *huge* tattoo of Latonya's name on her neck. *Some fathering he did!* Kadijah even returned with a nose and tongue piercing. *Following in the footsteps of Latonya I see!*

In my mind, I believed that Kadijah's relationship with Latonya was her first real sexual encounter and as a result, she did not know how to control her emotions. I suppose it was the lack of control that had my daughter behaving badly.

In any event, I took my daughter back in because, in all reality, I could not leave her out in the streets. That was for certain. The police even told me during one of their many visits to my house that I would be arrested if I abandoned her, so I took her back in that day. It did not take long for Kadijah to revert to her old ways. She once again started leaving the house and not returning. The calls to the police became so frequent that one officer pulled me to the side and gave me some of the best advice I had ever been given. He told me that I could have Kadijah arrested if I told an officer that she was a threat to others and herself. Meaning, if I told the officers she threatened to commit suicide, or harm someone in the house, she could be arrested and be removed from the house. Just like that, my plan for tough love started again. I only had to wait for the perfect opportunity.

One evening, my mother, Kadijah, Marquis, the younger kids and I were sitting in the living room watching a movie. Somehow a conversation came up between Kadijah and my mom where they did not agree with each other. The conversation was not serious until Kadijah jumped up from the couch and pushed my mother's ice cream cone into her hair and face. Understandably, my mother lost it, and a huge argument ensued between the two. I calmly got up from where I sat, walked over to the kitchen phone and dialed the police. I told them that my daughter threatened the life of both my mother and me, and that we were scared for our lives. Marquis had already taken his little sisters upstairs. He already knew the procedure. The police were at my door in what seemed like minutes, placing handcuffs on Kadijah. They could not take her to jail, but they could take her to Southside Hospital's Psych Unit. And that is precisely what they did. I thought my problems were over and done with, but once again I was wrong.

Once the officers checked Kadijah into the hospital, the hospital called me to say that I had to come and accompany my child. I learned that an underage child could not be in a hospital without a parent there to make sure everything was okay. *Cool. No problem.* I had no issue going to the hospital, but I was for damn sure not bringing her back home. While at Southside, the officer who brought Kadijah in told me that if I did not sign her out of the hospital they would transfer her to South Oaks Hospital, which is a psychiatric hospital. I let him know that option was fine with me and I had no plans on signing her out. She was going to reap what she had sown.

I remember sitting in the hospital waiting area and Kadijah begging me to take her home. Her crocodile tears meant nothing to me. I was at so much peace with my decision that I fell asleep and was awaken by an officer asking me to sign Kadijah's transport papers to South Oaks Hospital. I literally spent the night in the hospital and all for the sake of tough love. I was going to teach Kadijah a lesson if it was the last thing I did in life.

Once the papers were signed, I followed the transportation ambulance to South Oaks. Upon our arrival, I waited for the ambulance to bring her through the designated area before entering the hospital. Upon my entrance, I was directed to the main office, where I was greeted by a less than friendly receptionist and a ton of forms to fill out. In addition to all of the paperwork, I was told that I had to meet with the counselor who would handle Kadijah's case and the director of the youth program.

After I completed the numerous forms, I explained to the personnel all of the problems I was having with her. They felt it would be in my best interest to medicate Kadijah in an effort to calm her. I absolutely disagreed with them. Kadijah did not need to be medicated; she was simply disobedient. She was not crazy, although at times she acted like she was! The director let me know that Kadijah would only be able to stay in their facility for one week if I opted not to medicate her. That seemed reasonable, and I figured she would learn her lesson in a week's time.

I left the facility looking forward to a week without chaos. I wanted to enjoy time with my other three children, who were by now probably feeling neglected as a result of the constant attention Kadijah required. I wanted to fill our household with the positivity that was lacking due to Kadijah's drama and unneeded stress. The first thing I would do was take my children out for a bite to eat, and much needed time to unwind.

It did not take long for Kadijah to start calling the house promising to straighten up her act, but I did not want to hear any of it. She called on the second day of her stay at the hospital and begged me to come and get her. She felt that she did not belong in the hospital, particularly since she was with others who had very real and very scary issues. I let her know that because of her actions she was exactly where she belonged. I also let her know that her siblings were afraid to be around her. I told her that she had to deal with the consequences of her actions and I would see her at the end of the week. She was not happy and must have complained to her counselor because not even 24 hours after our conversation, I received a call from her counselor instructing me that it was my obligation to check on my child. I was undoubtedly displeased with this turn of events.

The counselor said he understood, but it did not change the fact that I needed to come and visit her.

Reluctantly, I visited her, but only for about 20 minutes. At the end of my visit she did not want me to leave; however, I was determined to show her the tough love that she needed. Before I knew it the week was over, and it was time for Kadijah to be released. She was so excited to be leaving and coming home. I did not know what had taken place at the facility, but whatever happened, it changed my child. Before we left, one of her counselors pulled me to the side and expressed that I had a good child. I told him he had no clue what I was up against, but he assured me that Kadijah was a changed person. It was no time at all before I could tell she was a different child and I liked it. She stopped bringing Latonya around, although the two were still seeing each other. For the most part, she was obeying the rules of the house and was doing well in school. I was ecstatic to see the change in her attitude and hoped that this time it would last.

With the newfound peace at home, I was able to concentrate on my work and my blog, HipHopGossipSite.com. It was doing well. My cousin Star, from the Star and Buc Wild Morning Show, even asked me to join his show to report on the latest industry rumors. I met Steph Lova, formerly of Hot 97 and Power 105 at a Lil Jon listening event at the DigiWaxx offices. I instantly liked her. We became fast friends, and she told me about an online internet radio show she was working on. The best part of it was that she wanted me to work on it with her. I was elated. I had a weekly slot on internet radio, from which I was able to shout out my site.

The friendship between Steph Lova and I continued to grow. We hosted events together, and her internet radio show began to grow. My career was blossoming as well. It was at an all-time high, and I was a part of three different internet radio shows at the same time. I met numerous celebrities and was having the time of my life! I could finally see that all of my hard work was paying off. I'm the first to admit that it was not always peaches and cream. The new work came with its own set of drawbacks. There were many times I had to bring my children to events with me. In order to stay ahead of the latest gossip, I even occasionally brought them with me to celebrity interviews. It was something I had to do to ensure that I was the first to report what was going on in the industry.

It was no secret, amongst anyone who knew me, that my oldest daughter was gay. Right before the eyes of anyone who cared to look, Kadijah's appearance transformed to one that outsiders often conventionally associated with lesbians. She had gone from a shapely girl with curls that flowed down her back, to cutting off her hair to embrace a more masculine appearance. I can't lie, it hurt me a bit when my Kadijah cut her hair because my baby always had such a gorgeous head of hair. But that was neither here nor there; it was what made her happy.

One day, I was at DTF studios in Brooklyn recording a weekly radio show with Steph Lova, when she mentioned something about Kadijah looking "hardcore." She was known for cracking jokes, and her words were not disrespectful, so we all laughed about it, Kadijah included. However, I was surprised when Kadijah shared with Steph Lova that she was considering changing her name to Kamal because she identified more with being a man.

That was the first time I ever heard her say something like that. And because I did not like what I was hearing; I ignored it. I did not want to make a big deal in front of people I did not know well. I left it alone and never entertained Kadijah's words because I thought she was losing her damn mind. I even thought about sending her back to counseling to deal with whatever it was she was going through. I did not understand her anymore, and she was clearly struggling with something.

After putting her comments off, I became sidetracked with work. I had received the news that I had the opportunity to be a part of a new reality show airing on VH1. On top of working my regular job and taking care of my kids, I was taking meetings with VH1 executives, including television producer Mona Scott-Young. I was excited by all of the things changing around me and before long Kadijah's comment about identifying more as a male was the furthest thing from my mind. I was preoccupied with getting my business in order because I was securing the reality show position if it was the last thing I did.

Not long after shooting a pilot for what would later become known as *The Gossip Game, I* received a call from Mona, with confirmation that VH1 had green lit the project. I, along with everyone else, was super excited. I was at work when I received the call, but that did not stop me from screaming into the phone. I was excited and grateful that with hard work, all of my dreams had finally come to fruition for the entire world to see. The call from Mona put me on cloud nine, and I was in no rush to ever come down.

The Gossip Game centered on seven women in the media industry and how they worked to obtain the latest rumors, gossip, and news. I was one of the bloggers on the show. I could not believe that little ole me would be working with and standing next to the likes of Angela Yee, Kim Osorio, and

Sharon Carpenter. My perception of the show soon changed, for the worse, when I discovered that my storyline would not solely focus on my work with my blog. Though it was not deliberate, my story would in time shift from my work to my child and her sexuality.

The beginning of the change stemmed from the amount of time I had to dedicate to filming *The Gossip Game*. Being as there are only but so many hours in a day, I started giving less attention to my internet radio shows. Due to the hectic nature of my schedule, I just could not maintain my previous dedication to them. I not only had to work at the hospital, but I had to film and make appearances to promote the show. Not to mention the commercials and hostings that had become a new part of my schedule. I was stretched thin, it took time away from, not only my internet radio shows but from my children and my nine-to-five as well. I was willing to risk my nine-to-five. Thankfully, I had a great husband who recognized the once in a lifetime opportunity before me and was willing to help more at home. I did not want to ruin my chance, so I accepted that there would be sacrifices to be made.

My relationship with Steph Lova started to deteriorate after an incident I had with fellow reality show stars I called 'Broke Pennies' and Erica Mena. My issue with Erica came about after I reported something about her on my blog that she did not like. Being as though we live in the age of social media, she took to her Twitter page to vent about me. Somehow or other, Broke Pennies involved himself by threatening me. In time, personal phone numbers were shared via social media and matters turned ugly. It goes without saying that I do not take too kindly to threats directed at me. So when I discovered that Steph Lova would be interviewing Broke Pennies for her show, I took the opportunity to bring every male I knew to Brooklyn so they could put him in his place. I was accompanied by approximately 18 people that day. I knew there was potential for things to go awry, but I did not care.

Luckily for Broke Pennies, he never showed to Steph Lova's show, but my actions caused her to feel a certain way. My gut tells me that she called Broke Pennies and advised him not to come up to the studio that day. I do not think she wanted him to assume that she was involved in what was sure to happen had he shown up. Not unexpectedly, she was not happy about what I did, but as a friend, she never said anything to me. She never once said, "Viv, what you are doing is wrong." It was no secret, and she had full knowledge of my issues with Broke Pennies. Either way, my actions bothered her to the point that we ended up not on speaking terms. I never imagined that there was a real problem between us. I just figured she was mad and would ultimately get over it, as friends who disagree often do. I soon found out just how wrong I was.

Steph Lova was never part of *The Gossip Game* cast. Be that as it may, she befriended Ms. Drama, a cast mate and fellow blogger on the show. For whatever reason, Ms. Drama hated me. It never made sense. I never stole any money from her, we never dated the same people, and I never said anything about anyone close to her. Why she did not like me was anyone's guess.

At any rate, rule number one in my book is if you are my friend at any point in time in life, you do not make friends with people I do not get along with. If you chose to do as such, you naturally become my enemy as well. That was the case with Steph Lova and I. I am sure if she was asked why our friendship fell apart, she more than likely would have another story to tell.

Following the demise of our friendship, rumors began to circulate around the entertainment industry that Steph Lova had fired me from her show. I knew that was impossible because last I checked a person had to be getting a paycheck in order to be fired. Since this did not apply to me, I paid the rumor no attention. My cousin Star who was to be interviewed on Steph Lova's internet radio show for VH1, decided to confront her about the rumors. The only problem was that he added his flair to the line of questions and put me squarely in the line of fire.

Star alluded to Steph Lova that I mentioned she was gay and tried to hit on me. She took real offense to Star's implications. She responded by stating she was not gay and I should know what gay was because my daughter was gay. This was one hundred percent the wrong thing to do; specifically from someone I thought was a friend. I knew we had our issues, but I never thought she would speak so recklessly about my child. She was someone who had invited my family to her daughter's birthday party; someone that I hung out with outside of the radio show as a friend. She was someone who confided in me and was definitely someone I thought had enough respect never to mention my child's name. Even if she hated me, I preferred that she kept her issues with me and me only; not my daughter. She never even bothered to contact me to verify if what Star said was true. This bothered me almost more than anything because she knew better than anyone that Star loved drama and the reactions he was able to elicit from others.

It hurt to hear what Steph Lova said about my daughter and on a public forum no less. But my anger surpassed any hurt I felt. How dare she disrespect my child? I was also angry with Star for starting the drama, and I was definitely mad at myself for not dealing with an issue I had placed on the back burner for so long. The time had come for me to address some very personal issues with my child. There was no time to waste. Not only were the streets talking, but VH1's camera had heard and seen it all. I was furious, and I wanted to fight someone. I wanted to hurt them the way my child would soon be hurt. The only question that ran through my mind was how could Steph Lova say that about my baby girl knowing she was being filmed? I struggled with the question until it dawned on me that it appeared that she always had a complex about not being feminine enough herself. It always bothered her when people had the slightest thought she may be gay. It pissed her off to no end; I remembered that much. So maybe Star's response, even though untrue, hit a nerve and she retaliated the only way she knew how.

At the conclusion of his interview, Star called to tell me everything that happened and how Steph

Lova reacted. He thought the way she carried on was funny, but I did not. Star had no idea what he started! VH1 and the good folks over at Magilla, the show's production company at the time, gained the much-needed traction they were looking for. And I was in the middle of all of it.

My primary concern was how I was going to tell Kadijah that Steph Lova dissed her on national television. I worried about this conversation being exposed to the public because I did not want to hear Kadijah talk about identifying with men. My worries only intensified when Mona called and asked me not to have any conversations with Kadijah regarding Steph Lova's comments. She wanted to get the conversation between Kadijah and me on camera, which was something that needed a lot of thought. I had not dealt with the situation in my private life and was not sure if I was ready for the world to watch me have that conversation with my child.

To complicate matters further and in true reality television fashion, Mona wanted me to film with Steph Lova to discuss her comments before I had the conversation with Kadijah! I was more than prepared to speak to her, on or off camera, but remained unsure about speaking with Kadijah. Although I knew I was to speak with Steph Lova, I did not know when the talk was scheduled. What many people do not know about reality television is even though we have a basic knowledge of what's going on, we are never told, on any given day, with whom we are filming. Producers merely send an email detailing the shoot date and location. There is also general guidance on how to appropriately dress for your scene.

After receiving one such email, intuition told me that I should investigate the pending scene further. I made a few calls to determine whether or not I was filming with Angela Yee, Kim Osorio or Sharon Carpenter; the cast mates I got along with. When each of them informed me that they were not filming that day, I automatically knew that I would be filming with Steph Lova. It just made sense, and there was no other logical scenario. When the shoot date arrived, I surveyed the location to confirm my suspicions. Sure enough, there were multiple security guards. That was all the verification I needed. I was definitely filming with her. I then parked in a nearby garage and headed toward the shooting location.

As I walked, I prepared for what I knew was to come. I opted to forgo the usual pre-shoot beauty routine offered by VH1. Typically, before filming takes place, the network would ensure that the cast's hair and makeup were nicely done. All things considered, I asked my makeup artist for the day to keep everything light. I reasoned that if I had to fight, I did not need makeup smeared all over my face on camera. I looked in the mirror at my hair and asked my makeup artist if I could borrow his brush. He was concerned that I did not like how he had styled me, but I reassured him that was not the case. I told him I would be putting my hair in a doobie, a style created by wrapping my hair tightly around my head. I knew that there was a great possibility that my day included a fight and did not want my hair getting in the way. Word had traveled fast around the staff and production regarding Steph Lova's comments on Kadijah, and many of them were not pleased with her. He looked at me for a moment, told me he understood; but not before trying his best to talk me out of styling my hair for battle. It was of no use, and he knew my mind was set. He knowingly handed me the brush, and I styled my hair.

I wrapped my hair up nice and tight, and held it precisely in place with all of my bobby pins. I then waited for filming to begin. Mona walked into the venue to check on me. Upon realizing that my hair was not down, she questioned me as to why I was not ready. I told her that I was ready and if she was going to be filming my reality, what she saw was what it was going to be. I expressed to Mona that I knew I would be filming with Steph Lova and I was going to film exactly how I was; in light makeup and a doobie. Mona gently guided me outside into one of the vans that typically held cast members until it was their time to film. Once inside the van, she asked the driver to take us for a brief ride. Mona turned to me and began to speak earnestly. She told me that she had no intention to use the footage of Steph Lova commenting on

Kadijah. I was not so easily convinced and had no problem letting her know that my knowledge of the situation was directly from the horse's mouth. A silence fell over the van. Mona stared at me for what seemed like forever; as if she was shocked I had spoken to her in that manner. I was the first to break the silence. I expressed that it was not fair for Steph Lova to be able to say something like that about my child and go unpunished. "An eye for an eye," was and always will be fair play. Our conversation continued, each of us making our points. We may not have agreed on everything, but it was undeniable that my storyline had completely changed. I silently wondered what happened to the original premise of the show. What happened to capturing 'Vivian the Hustler,' gossip blogger extraordinaire? I found myself feeling like reality television was a joke, and the joke was on me.

By the end of our conversation, the topic of discussion shifted to my hair. Mona inquired why I had put my hair in a doobie. I calmly explained that I was being proactive in the event that there was a physical altercation while filming. Mona insisted that nothing would happen since security was on hand to stop anything before it happened. I did not want to take any chances. I would rather be safe than sorry! There was no chance that I would let anyone catch me off guard. My hair was staying exactly as it was.

Mona continued to attempt to persuade me to take my hair down, but finally relented when she realized that no amount of asking would change my mind. She resigned to let me have my way and accepted that I would film with my hair wrapped. But before we parted ways and exited the van, she shared that Steph Lova wanted to apologize for her comments regarding Kadijah. I was shocked. *Why now? Why did she suddenly want to apologize?* I knew her all too well, and I was positive she had no intentions of apologizing. Mona did not know her the way I did. Therefore, I took her thoughts on the apology with a grain of salt.

We concluded our discussion, exited the van and walked onto set prepared to confront Steph Lova. The production staff led me to an empty bar, cleared of any glasses and utensils. I have no doubt this was to keep potential weapons out of my grasp. It was only me, the bar and two stools; one of which was for Steph Lova. Though there were two stools, I had absolutely no plans of sitting down. I was going to stand up the entire time we filmed, and nothing was going to change that. Cameras started to roll, and I waited for her to pay me a visit.

She walked in, her eyes hidden behind darkened sunglasses. At the mere sight of her, I was ready to pounce. But Mona had asked that I allow for at least three minutes of dialogue; therefore I obliged. The sound of my husband's voice rang in my head. It was as if I could hear him mocking me for not being able to at least let Steph Lova walk into the room before I attacked. This was enough to momentarily calm me down. It was then that I noticed she was dressed as if she were coming to see an old friend. Her hair was down, she had applied makeup, and she even wore a purse. Her expression conveyed her surprise that I was dressed with other plans in mind. Her mood instantly changed. Where her face once wore a smile sat a frown.

We began speaking, yet an apology never escaped her lips. All I heard was finger pointing and blame shifting. I grew angrier the more she spoke. I had no interest in anything she said, considering none of it involved an apology. Before I knew it, our voices were raised and my visceral reaction was to spit at her; right in her face. Spitting was the nastiest, most vile way I could show her the same lack of respect she had shown my child. I no longer cared about any dialogue, taping, or the show in general. I waited for her to react, to lunge at me in some form, so I could release the anger that had been festering in me since she disrespected Kadijah. Surprisingly, she never made a move in my direction. She sat motionless for a brief moment and then stood from her stool. *Why wasn't she coming for me after I spat at her?* I then realized Steph Lova wasn't anything but talk. She was just mad because she incorrectly assumed I was telling people that she was gay.

By the time security intervened the looming threat of a fight had passed. She and I continued to exchange words and promised that *we would see each other again*. Ultimately, we went our separate ways. Being as I had completed filming for the day, Mona and a few security guards escorted me out of the building and into the same van from earlier. She and a few other producers attempted to calm me down with the hopes of getting me to film with her again. *They had to be joking. Did Mona just ask me to film with her again? Today? Nah; it wasn't happening.* I had already given her what she wanted and began to feel as if she wanted more than I was willing to give. I just did not have it in me. No amount of money would make me return to set to speak to her again. As far as I was concerned, Steph Lova no longer existed. She was dead to me.

Coincidentally, of all of the days, Kadijah and Latonya came to set to meet me. Sensing my mood, they asked what was wrong. I had no choice but to tell Kadijah that Steph Lova had made negative comments about her being gay on national television. I also did not hesitate to share that I wanted to rip her face off for making those reckless comments. Kadijah calmly replied, "Why are you so mad at her about that? Steph Lova is talking about Kadijah, and I'm not Kadijah. I'm Kamal." *Kamal? I thought to myself.*

I let Kadijah's statement go in one ear and out of the other. I was too angry to process what she had said. She would never know what I was going through until she had a child of her own. Furthermore, Mona was in the van, and I did not want to get into an argument with my child in front of her. The fact that I was irritated from my previous encounter with Steph Lova did nothing to improve the atmosphere in the van. So I did the only thing I could do; I left the set and went home.

Mona called me the following day to check on me and was pleased to find out I was feeling better. A few minutes into our conversation she advised me to prepare to film with Kadijah within the coming days. I would be lying if I said I was looking forward to discussing private matters on camera for her and the entire world to see. My emotions ran high in nervous anticipation and remained unwilling to confront them head on. Nevertheless, I assured Mona that I would properly prepare myself and hung up the phone.

Honestly, I did not understand Kadijah. And I could not fathom what it felt like to be something I was not. I had long ago accepted that she was gay, but I was genuinely confused when Kadijah shared that she thought she was a boy. I know for a fact that years ago I birthed a baby girl. I began to openly question if I had done something wrong or made an error in how I chose to raise her. Was I not a good enough parent? Did someone inappropriately touch her when she was younger, and I did not know? Did she hate women? Did she hate men? All of these questions and more, regardless of rationale, ran through my mind and I needed answers. Yet, I had serious reservations about asking them on camera. Kadijah, on the other hand, was excited to have the conversation filmed. She wanted people to know who she was. I, on the other hand, second guessed my decision ever to join the show.

Two days later, Mona, a camera crew, and several VH1 executives arrived at my front door ready to film Kadijah and me. A sense of dread hung over me, and I was a ball of nerves. I had never been as nervous as I was waiting for Mona to cue the scene. I reminded myself to not show any anger, all while willing myself not to cry. In the middle of my pep talk, Mona walked over with instructions for Kamal and me. *Kamal?* Surely my ears deceived me. She could not have possibly addressed my child as Kamal, and not Kadijah. I later found out the two of them spoke frequently, and Mona was very familiar with how my child was feeling. Mona's remaining instructions broke me from my thoughts. Above the pounding of my heart, I heard the words, "Tell her what's on your mind. And Vivian, I want you to listen."

I could not believe I was being told how I was allowed to react. Couldn't everyone see that I was confronting a topic I was not quite ready to face? What if I did not want to listen? What if I wanted to lash out? I excused myself to the bathroom in an attempt to regain my composure. As the door closed behind, I turned on the water to drown out the background noise that surrounded me. I did not want to take the chance of overhearing someone speaking badly about me. I took a few deep breaths, splashed my face with water and said a quick prayer for guidance. I prayed that God would take control of my tongue, and not allow me to say the wrong things. I also prayed for the strength to make it through the day.

Upon concluding my prayer, I walked out of the bathroom and headed toward the couch to sit next to my child. Seconds later, Mona asked if we were ready to film. We both nodded yes, but neither of us spoke right away. Kadijah was the first to break the silence. She confessed she had given the Steph Lova situation much thought, and appreciated why it angered me. She spoke with a maturity beyond her years when she expressed that she sensed my discomfort and understood my reasons for never broaching the topic of her sexuality. The subject then shifted to Steph Lova, who she deemed unworthy of my continued anger.

Kadijah went on to explain that she harbored no ill will toward Steph Lova because the comments she made were directed at Kadijah, and she was not Kadijah. My child proceeded to share that her outward appearance did not match who she truly was inside. Moreover, it frustrated her to no end, when I blew off her previous attempts to tell me that she was tired of living a lie. She wanted nothing more than to live in her truth. She was not a young lady named Kadijah; *"he"* was a young man named Kamal.

Tears streamed down my face, and I was no longer able to heed Mona's advice to listen. My breakdown was swift and uncontrollable. I sobbed in front of everyone; Mona, the camera crew and the executives. I could not stop; I could not speak. A lump formed in my throat and I felt as if I could not breathe. Just hours earlier, I thought my lesbian daughter was in the middle of a juvenile phase. I realized that might have been the reason I chose to ignore many of the signs she tried to show me. But since she had my undivided attention, she was not holding anything back. The first words I said through my tears were an apology. If nothing else, I owed my child that. I struggled to speak but managed to express how much I loved her, and I was her mother regardless of what happened moving forward. I may not have had all of the right words, but it was paramount that my child heard that I loved her irrespective of everything. Nothing else mattered to me as long as my child knew she was loved!

Were her words easy to digest? No, they were not. Did I one hundred percent understand the situation right away? Again, no I did not. What I did know was, in spite of everything, I needed to be there for my child. I had not realized, until that moment, just how much she needed me. I was not there for her for a long time and knowing this made me feel horrible. The last thing I ever wanted to do was allow any of my children to feel as if I did not love them or care about their lives. I could not stop apologizing and showered my baby with hugs.

The scene VH1's cameras caught was absolutely real. All of the emotion and tears were genuine. I was raw and vulnerable in front of millions. The nation bore witness, as I released years of pent up frustration. When it was all said and done, and production had wrapped, several crew members and a producer told me they were proud of me. They shared stories of their sexuality and the issues it created with family members. I found some comfort in their words. Despite the nagging feeling I had made a fool of myself in front of the world, I started to feel like I could breathe again. Eventually, Mona and the crew packed up and left. For the rest of the day, I spent time with Kadijah, learning more about how she felt inside.

Over the course of our heart-to-heart, she spoke of becoming aware in her adolescence that she liked girls and how, even then, she did not see herself as everybody else saw her. She said she knew she was different then, but did not know how to tell anyone. I was honest when I told her that I had long ago accepted that she was gay. The fact that she was attracted to girls did not bother me at all. Be that as it may, I just was not sure how ready I was to accept that my daughter had become my son. It confused and scared me. Nothing made any sense. When I looked at my child, I saw a beautiful young lady standing before me. One that I birthed and loved; yet she was not happy with who she was. Although it was not an affront to me, it hurt that my child no longer wished to be called by the name I had affectionately given her. It was difficult to face that she no longer wanted to be addressed as Kadijah, but instead as Kamal. It was all so new, and I implored Kadijah to be patient with me.

My mind, once again, returned to what I may have done wrong as a parent and how I carried myself in her presence. Was it my fault? Did I expose my baby to too much when she was younger? Worst of all, did my child not like me to the point that she would rather live her life as a man rather to risk being like me? My thoughts raced from the logical to illogical until I became dizzy. I was overwhelmed, and there was no one I could talk to. I feared my significant other would not understand and my friends would judge my child. I indisputably could not talk to Kadijah's father because he could not be bothered regardless of her gender. Just as during her birth, I felt alone; and did not know where to turn. The result of my perceived solitude was more questions, to which I was not sure I would ever have the answers.

Maybe Kadijah was affected by me having her so young? Did my age impede her mental development? The questions were never-ending, and I began to debate my decision to go against the doctor's suggestion to have her medicated. Did she need to start taking medication? I just did not know, and all of the woulda, coulda, shouldas did not change that. I was not prepared in the least, and it seemed like I was standing stagnant, while everything around me moved at the speed of light. Specifically, once my child revealed that she was seriously considering taking testosterone. *Testosterone!*

Granted I had never been too religious, but I always both loved and feared God. To hear that my child was changing herself from what He created frightened me. Kadijah shared with me that she had been seeing a doctor in the Bronx who spoke with her in detail about her feelings. His recommendation was for her to start taking testosterone. I was livid! Kadijah was only 17, a minor, and would not be taking testosterone until I approved it. Who exactly did this doctor think he was to make such a recommendation without so much as consulting me?

The new revelation rocked me to my core, and I worried about how I would handle the new admission. I was rapidly losing any semblance of control and felt helpless. The reality of the situation was that Kadijah would soon be a legal adult and would no longer have to seek my advice or approval. I was at a loss and once again pushed my issues to the back of my mind with the hope they would disappear. Naturally, that was not the case.

With each passing day, I watched Kadijah gradually disappear. Slowly, her voice deepened, and her mannerisms became more like those associated with masculinity. Her style evolved and her clothes were noticeably different. She no longer wore perfume; her chosen scent began to be selected from various colognes. Her excitement to take testosterone became palpable, and the anticipation of its arrival in the mail was almost too much for me to bear. It was one of the last steps in transitioning and her finally feeling like who she was born to be.

The inevitable was rapidly approaching and the closer it got, the more scared I became. Complicating matters further was the fact that I was in the middle of taping *The Gossip Game*. The day came when I was notified that I was needed for taping. Any apprehension and nervousness that I previously felt eased when I learned that I was to tape with Kim Osorio. Kim is incredibly cool and, like me, is a mother. Because of this, I related to her a little more than my other cast mates, and we almost instantaneously clicked. She was like a big sister to me, one who was encouraging and always kept an open mind. Kim's vibe was amazing and just good to be around.

For the scene in question, Kim and I were to meet for lunch to have a friendly conversation and to catch up with each other. As it was with every other scene I filmed, producers provided us with a topic of discussion from which our conversations were supposed to flow. As one could imagine, I was informed that we were to discuss Kadijah, her transition, and my feelings on her changing her name to Kamal. In all honesty, I was not ready to discuss Kadijah with anyone, but if I had to, I was glad that it was with Kim.

Even still, I was utterly tired of discussing her for the entertainment of others. Furthermore, I was endlessly frustrated filming scenes that had strayed so far from my original purpose. I had not signed up for the world to bear witness to my personal life. I began to feel like my sole purpose on the show was to be one person who was always involved in drama. Producers no longer wanted to film me conducting celebrity interviews; nor did they want to film all of the hard work I put in building my brand. The only footage they were interested in capturing was me talking about Steph Lova, who was irrelevant in me and my child's life. I was tired of giving the world and the production company all of me for just four thousand dollars an episode. My life, my turmoil, and my child were worth more than that. But as they say in the entertainment world, the show must go on. So in an act of fortitude, I told Kim that while I was dealing with a lot, I was okay to film the scene.

The day of filming ended and after my on camera discussion with Kim, I was once again at a familiar crossroads when it came to Kadijah. I loved my child, but I was not too happy with the decisions being made. In the following days, I found myself checking the mail, every day without fail, to see if the testosterone arrived. I planned to throw the entire package promptly into the garbage can. One day, I opened the mailbox, and there sat a nondescript white box addressed to Kadijah. Without a second thought, I knew right away exactly what the box held: the testosterone. I snatched it from the mailbox and brought it into the house with every intention of it joining the day's trash. But then I began to think. I contemplated the range of emotions and life-long decisions contained inside the small white box. I thought about all that its contents meant for both my child and me. I knew it would bring happiness to my child, which is any mother's truest wish. However, to me, I knew it would only bring confusion and heartache. I sat paralyzed; frozen by my pending decision. I was at a loss. The only thing clear to me was that I could not reach a decision as to the fate of the package on my own. I closed my eyes and began to pray. I spoke to God and sincerely asked for guidance because I was more lost than I had ever been. He sent an answer as I sat with a tear stained face. His answer was clear, and as if it had been in front of me the entire time. I realized if I prevented Kadijah from taking the testosterone, she, who was just shy of being a legal adult, would more than likely either take it behind my back or wait until she no longer needed my approval. There was also the grand possibility that eventually she would stop sharing her life with me for fear that if I disagreed I would intervene or somehow prohibit her wishes. The worst and most plausible possibility was that my child would at some point grow to resent me. So, I placed the box on the dining room table with a note telling her she had mail. As a parent, it was probably one of the hardest things I ever had to do, but I did it. I was scared, but I did it. I was angry and upset, but I did it. Not for me, but for my child; because our relationship was infinitely more important than my feelings. Besides, my feelings were nothing more than a brief and fleeting reaction. Irrespective of what I was feeling at that moment, I would eventually get over it. With a brief glance in the direction of the white box, I walked out of the house and prayed for the best.

In due course, Kadijah began taking testosterone. I did not instantly see any real physical changes; however, I did notice that her voice deepened. Initially, it was strange, if for no other reason than occasionally not being able to differentiate between the speaking voices of Marquis and Kadijah. By this time she begged me to address her as Kamal, which I reluctantly did after much effort. The switch was harder than I would have ever imagined. I had addressed my child as Kadijah for over 17 years, so that name flowed naturally from my lips whenever I spoke;

therefore, I had to reteach myself what to call my child.

In the meantime, filming for *The Gossip Game* had not yet ended, and I had to film once more with Steph Lova. To put it mildly, I was not looking forward to being in her vicinity, even though I was once again informed that I was due an apology. Not unexpectedly, the apology never happened, and our encounter was unproductive. I do not remember much about that day, but I recall telling myself that if I never spoke to Steph Lova again, it would be too soon. I was done with her, and I was done with the show. There would be no more filming, no more someone telling me what to talk about, and no more outsiders making my life difficult.

Although the time for filming had thankfully passed, making event appearances and hostings did not. I was busier than ever. Amid it all, I received a call from my former cast mate Angela Yee asking if I would bring Kadijah to Power 105's *The Breakfast Club,* a syndicated radio show based in New York City and hosted by her, DJ Envy, and

Charlamagne Tha God. I agreed, and Kadijah, who by that time had told everyone she was Kamal, was excited to tell the world the same. At that point, addressing my child as Kamal was no longer a problem. It was "she" and "her" versus "he" and "him" that was a bit difficult. I was not getting it right, albeit unintentionally, and Kamal would have to correct me consistently. This made me nervous because I did not want to run the risk of using the incorrect pronoun, or even worse calling my child Kadijah instead of Kamal, in front of millions of listeners. Truthfully, I was nervous about appearing on *The Breakfast Club* altogether and almost completely changed my mind about the interview.

VH1 aired the episode of *The Gossip Game* with Kamal's revelation the night before our scheduled appearance. And while I was overjoyed to have received an outpouring of love from supporters, I could not ignore the fact that I also received threats and hate email. Many of the comments on my social media pages were from vicious people who were unhappy with my support of Kamal's transition. The vile nature of the behavior and comments I received only furthered my apprehension for the interview. I was not ready for Kamal to face how cruel the world could be, especially when they hid behind a computer screen. Even with my misgivings, I could not overlook that Kamal was excited beyond measure, and frankly, I did not want to upset or disappoint him. So I did the only thing I could do to make the situation better. I prepared by anticipating questions and practicing my responses to gauge how quickly I was able to respond.

The next morning, I instinctively opened my eyes and rolled over to check the time to see I had overslept. I was unsure how that was possible being as I was a ball of nerves. Nonetheless, it happened. I jumped out of bed, woke Kamal, and the two of us scrambled to get dressed before heading for our interview. The ride from Long Island to Manhattan, where *The Breakfast Club* records, was a task as usual; however I was thankful for the extra time to prepare Kamal. I warned him that host, Charlamagne Tha God, was notorious for asking hard hitting questions that seem to sometimes come out of left field, but always went for the jugular. Although I knew Charlamagne to be a very nice person outside of radio, I was well aware that he had a job to do once the microphone turned on and I did not want Kamal to be offended. It was just business, and I wanted Kamal to fully understand before we walked into the studio. There was no way I was going to let my child be blindsided. Amazingly, and with more maturity than I could have ever imagined, Kamal said he knew what Charlamagne was about and did not care what he was going to ask. I released a deep sigh of relief and basked in the pride I felt for my son. His bravery was unmatched, despite living in a hateful and merciless world. Although I would always be his biggest protector, I was certain that Kamal would face a lifetime of challenges simply because he chose to be himself. I wanted more than anything to protect my child from those who wished him harm in any form. It was my prayer for him since birth, especially since he began his transition. And it was my prayer again, in the car, on the way to *The Breakfast Club*. I did not want listeners to see my child as anything other than the wonderful person he is. So I prayed that listeners would not think of Kamal as a freak. I also prayed that they would not see me as a terrible parent. More importantly, I prayed the interview would open the eyes and hearts of listeners while educating those who may not have understood the transgender community.

Once Kamal and I reached Power 105's studios, I called Angela Yee and told her we were waiting in the downstairs lobby. We waited patiently, all while I could hear my heart beat increase with nervous energy. I willed myself to calm down. Conversely, my anticipation continued to swell gradually. It was not my environment that brought about the battle with my nerves. I was more than comfortable at the studio and with everyone there because this was not my first time as a guest on *The Breakfast Club*. But this time was different; I was there with my child. This was the thought that replayed in my mind until an intern came to escort Kamal and me upstairs. When the elevator doors parted, we were warmly greeted by Angela Yee, who then ushered us into the booth with her, DJ Envy and Charlamagne Tha God.

We were not in the booth long before the interview began and DJ Envy introduced Kamal and me. And just like that my nervousness subsided. That's not to say that my earlier concerns were no longer valid, it was just that at that moment I began to worry less and focused more so on the opportunity Kamal had before him. I listened closely as Angela Yee recapped the previous night's episode of *The Gossip Game*, including my not so subtle interaction with Steph Lova. In spite of that ill-fated turn of events, Angela shared that she thought my scenes with Kamal were heartfelt. Then she graciously asked if we preferred her to refer to Kamal as my son or my daughter; to which I naturally replied, "My son." Instantly I softened. That one unassuming and modest question was immeasurably beautiful, and I sincerely appreciated the consideration and respect it showed for Kamal. And with that,

Angela, DJ Envy, and Charlamagne delved further into our interview.

As anticipated, the first question revolved around the previous night's episode of *The Gossip Game,* including how the relationship between Steph Lova and I reached the point of no return. I summarized our once-friendly turned tumultuous relationship, ending with Steph Lova's unfortunate attempt to embarrass Kamal. To my surprise, Kamal interjected and clarified that he was neither gay nor my daughter. I was taken aback, not because he had corrected me, but it was one of the first times that he had publicly defended himself. My heart swelled as Kamal confirmed that he was perfectly capable of speaking up for himself. However, I was at a loss for words. My reply was, "Yeah I know, but people do not understand what you mean when you say that." And just like that, the door was opened to a frank and honest discussion about what it meant for Kamal to be transgender.

DJ Envy asked Kamal to explain further both his comment and what "made him want to transition to a male." Like me, he recognized this as Kamal's opportunity to educate an audience who at the time may have never engaged with another transgender person. While doing so was in no way Kamal's responsibility, his words could go a long way in enlightening *The Breakfast Club's* listeners. I sat quietly as Kamal began to speak. He responded that he was born biologically a female, but was transitioning to be a male. To which Charlamagne replied, "You're doing the Chaz Bono thing?" Kamal began to speak, but then he took an almost imperceptible moment before speaking again. Listeners could not see the change in his demeanor, but those in the booth witnessed as Kamal's posture became slightly defensive. His inherent response and true feelings to Charlamagne's question read over his entire face. Kamal was clearly not happy with the comparison, and I was perplexed by his reaction to the seemingly innocent correlation. Kamal quietly, yet emphatically, replied that Chaz Bono was not someone he looked up to because he believed that Chaz unnecessarily complicated the lives of other transgender individuals by making it difficult for them to receive assistance with obtaining sex realignment surgery.

Although I had forewarned Kamal that he may be asked questions he did not like, the shift in his mood was obvious. In an effort to restore the earlier vibe, DJ Envy implored Kamal not to take anything personally because the topic was one that the deejays were not exceptionally familiar. He continued to state that they were all doing their best to learn more and were merely trying to understand. DJ Envy's words put Kamal at ease and carried on to express the sentiment he began before the mention of Chaz Bono. Kamal explained that there was nothing that made him "want" to be male. I would be lying if I said his answer did not surprise me because from my vantage point it seemed like that was all Kamal wanted to talk about lately. A day would not go by that he did not talk about transitioning or his hormones. Kamal proceeded to clarify his statement. The reason why there was nothing that made him want to be male was because until recently he had not fully understood himself. For as long as he could remember, he thought dressing like a man and having a romantic interest in women was what life held for him. That was until he researched and discovered everything he had experienced, and all that he felt classified him as a transgender person; leading him to begin hormone replacement therapy.

Charlamagne once again interrupted to raise an entirely ill-timed and inappropriate question. "You mean you can buy a penis?" he asked. Even though I expected nothing less from him, I audibly gasped and whispered Charlamagne's name beneath my breath. Kamal, on the other hand, remained calm. He responded that one could indeed buy a prosthetic, or they had the option to get genital reconstruction surgery. Charlamagne's interest was piqued, or at least it seemed so, and the interview took an unpredictable turn. He inquired if Kamal opted for surgery would his penis "feel like the real thing." At that point, it was safe to say that the conversation was one that I was uncomfortable participating in. Though I knew reconstruction surgery was always an option, I was in the beginning stages of recognizing what being transgender meant for Kamal. Although I fully accepted his next steps, I did not want to hear about his surgery. He was my child, and like most mothers, I was apprehensive of any medical procedure my son may have. Sensing my uneasiness, Charlamagne lightened the conversation by sharing that he would have to go out and buy himself some more inches and girth. Of course, everyone laughed. With a smile on my face, I said a little prayer of thanks because in the words of Kevin Hart...I wasn't ready!

Soon after the laughter dwindled down, DJ Envy redirected the conversation to my feelings as a mother of a transgender son. He was curious about my perspective on having given birth to Kadijah and now being the mother of Kamal. I let them know that even as Kadijah, I knew for a long time that my child was different from the other little girls. In my explanation, I referred to Kamal as "she" and said "her" a few times. Without any reservation or one care in the world, Kamal swiftly corrected me on air. It was a magnificent display of self-confidence observed by everyone in the room. DJ Envy asked if I called Kamal "he" now. To which I replied, "I have to because he corrects me." Before I could complete my sentence, Charlamagne said, "He's not having it!" And at that moment, the bond between Kamal and Charlamagne was born.

We continued to discuss other matters before the interview came to an end. All in all, it went well. Most of my fears were thankfully unfounded. I could breathe again because I had walked away from *The Breakfast Club* interview feeling more confident than ever in my support of Kamal. The five of us commemorated the occasion with pictures, after which Kamal and I returned to Long Island. I arrived home to congratulatory calls from many of my friends commending how well I handled the interview. Their sentiments fell in line with the words DJ Envy shared before I left the studio. He was proud of how I was handling, not only Kamal's transition but also finding out he was transgender. DJ Envy openly wondered how he would manage such news.

Each parent is different, and I can only assume that it's not a typical conversation most are prepared for until they have a transgender child. However, it's hard to imagine, a parent, despite any surprise or lack of understanding, not being there for their child. When I publicly speak of my life as a parent of a transgender son, the stories I hear are heartbreaking. Most involve children confiding their innermost thoughts to their parents and those same parents, the ones who are supposed to be there for them and protect them, react by kicking them out of the family home and disowning them. I can't fathom having ever done this to any of my children. In my eyes, children are a blessing and a gift from The Almighty. They did not ask to be brought into this world. It was a decision that we, as parents, made for them. Our gift back to God is how we raise them, and the values we instill in them. The fact of the matter is my love for my children comes without condition. I love them for everything they are, in spite of anything they do and in the face of all that may come. It's quite possible that I will be disappointed with some of their decisions, behaviors or life choices. But it will never negate my love for them.

After *The Breakfast Club* interview I unwittingly, though happily, became someone others turned to on the topic of being the parent of a transgender child. I was often called to speak on various panels in the wake of tragedies in the transgender community. I even garnered the attention of the Reverend Al Sharpton. Because of my openness and willingness to speak and listen, I became a mediator of sorts for parents who were having difficulties after learning their child was transgender. I was, and continue to be, a listening ear and shoulder to cry on because although I understood parents' frustrations, I also sympathized with what the children were going through. I never fail to point out to parents that life can be brutal and oftentimes one's home offers refuge from all that seeks to destroy their child's spirit. I remind them that home is where one goes for comfort, love, and peace. So why then should their child, transgender or cisgender, be subjected to persecution in their own home? Why make your child's life miserable because you may not understand what it's like to be transgender? I implore parents, regardless of the level of understanding or stage of acceptance, to first and foremost, just be there for their child.

Initially, I did not realize how therapeutic speaking out in the community would be. That was until I noticed when I spoke out about an issue I was having regarding Kamal, the better and more comfortable I would feel. The more I spoke, the more others communicated how much I helped them in one way or another. Thus, when Reverend Al Sharpton and the National Action Network requested that Kamal and I speak to a community rocked by the heinous murder of a transgender woman, we decidedly obliged.

Kamal and I sat on the panel, and I listened intently as everyone spoke until the time arrived for me to address the crowd. I looked out into the sea of faces, unsure what comfort I could bring in light of the tragedy. I opened my mouth, and my experience as a parent who early on struggled with their transgender child filled the air. I explained to those gathered that the acceptance I had for my child was not an easy road by any means. I sought counseling to better understand Kamal when the things he did did not make any sense to me. I shared that it was through Allah's mercy that I was able to open up my heart, ears, and mind to see past my understanding. And in a move that may have upset some of the transgender men and women in attendance, I asked that they have empathy for their parents. Though parents and children are on opposite sides of the experience, parents also need time to process and navigate emotions for which they may not be initially prepared. It's a process for both parent and child.

As I continued, I spoke of Kamal's transition to male and declared that I loved my child whether he was Kamal or Kadijah. This statement outraged some of the audience, or at the very least one person, because someone angrily yelled out that I had outed my child. I became immediately defensive and my attitude reflected as such. Who was this stranger to tell me I outed anyone? I felt my irradiation steadily increase, that is until Kamal stepped in. He informed the crowd that I was new in my acceptance and that I occasionally messed up when addressing him. But it was not out of malice or lack of caring. His words soothed the crowd, and they realized neither Kamal nor I were the enemy. Instead, we were both there with love and to give a little insight into how others think. As we stood side by side speaking, Kamal and I grew tighter by the minute. My child, who was once very disrespectful, had metamorphosed before my eyes. Whereas in the past he would have stood idly by, he now came to my defense. I appreciated him for that more than he would ever know.

Our interactions with one another showed that indifferent of everything, I had my child's best interests at heart and he, in turn, had mine. The crowd saw firsthand, and I am confident they sensed the genuine growth we had as a family. Before Kamal and I left the stage, Reverend Sharpton shared the touching story of his sister, who was a member of the LGBTQ community. Her story was one of struggle, hardship, and in the end, triumph. It demonstrated if a person stays positive, and in prayer, things will eventually work out. Though the people were different and the scenario was not exactly the same; the story was that of Kamal and me.

Once the panel discussion concluded, Kamal and I mingled with the crowd and members of the National Action Network. I soon learned there were a number of people both gay and transgender waiting to speak to me. I had no doubt they all wanted to give me a piece of their minds. Surprisingly, that was not the case at all. Instead, many of them shared the traumatizing experience of coming out or revealing that they were transgender to their parents. Each person spoke of believing if they lived and shared their truths, they would feel better about themselves. Regrettably, each person that spoke was wrong. They shared stories of reactions that included abandonment, homelessness, and physical abuse. One person told me that when he revealed to his mom that he was gay, she kicked him out of the house.

The misfortune in their stories seemed to be endless, and while they spoke, all I could think about was how horrible it was to suffer for being who you were born to be. It was a horrible reality that I would not wish on anyone, especially at the hands of their parents. I could not understand it and questions ran rampant through my mind. *How can a parent do this to their child? How can one choose a stranger over their child? How can someone beat their child to a pulp, and think the child deserved it?* The stories put my life into perspective. Until hearing their stories, I thought Kamal and I had gone through the worst of it. Our version of events was mild in comparison, and for that we were grateful. It was a reminder that if we ever thought we are having a bad day, there was always someone having a worse one. Kamal and I went home that night and prayed together.

Subsequent to the event with Reverend Sharpton, Kamal and I had a number of speaking engagements. After our commitments began to die down slowly, we took the time to work on our relationship. I also took the time to work on me. By this time, Kamal's voice had significantly deepened, more so than before, and there were times when hearing him speak would make me cry. I always hid my tears from him, because I would never want him to think they represented my opposition to his transition. In fact, my tears were not for Kamal at all; they were for me. Even though I loved and accepted him with all of my heart, there was a small part of me that was just beginning to realize that my little girl was no more. And in those times, I wondered how my life would have been if some of my life decisions had been different.

I would long for the three wishes granted by a genie trapped in his lamp. With my wishes, I would change the fact that I lost my virginity to an abusive jerk who would later become an absentee father. I would also make sure not to have my children around nonsense. But in life, there are no genies or no do overs. We deal with what God places before us, we endure, and we survive. So the life I had, with all of its pain and joy; triumphs and defeats; and mistakes and accomplishments, was mine. I could not change the past any more than I could change the world. The only thing I could change was me. I could change how I thought, how I reacted and how I carried myself. I could change who I welcomed into my home, who I chose as friends, and how I spoke to others. And when I made these changes in me, everything around me changed for the better. My relationships, especially with Kamal, improved. I communicated much more clearly with others, and my daily interactions were altogether more pleasant.

My life began to fall in place to the extent that when Kamal shared that he wanted to have his breast removed after almost a year of incessantly binding them, I handled it much better than I would have previously. At a size 34 DD, Kamal was very busty and had the daily task of binding his breast with an Ace bandage. It was an unpleasant and often painful task, but he did it every single day; even in the scorching heat of the New York summer. It was agony for him. He never wore any tank tops or tight fitting shirts for the fear that someone might detect his breasts. My heart went out to my son because I knew he was just plain tired of his breast. He was tired of having to wear a binder; he was tired of being uncomfortable, and he was tired of feeling like he had to hide his body. I was scared for Kamal because surgery, even for a good reason, is still surgery and held the possibility of complications. However, he was adamant; therefore, I placed whatever apprehension I had about the surgery on the back burner. Though I supported him, I nevertheless, advised him to do his research before jumping headfirst into anything. He had to find a surgeon with impeccable credentials, great patient referrals and most importantly, a surgeon who was board certified to perform chest masculinization surgery.

It took Kamal approximately a good two months to find a surgeon he felt was right to perform his surgery. The downside being the surgeon was located in Ohio. Ohio?! Not New York? Not New Jersey? But in speaking with Kamal, I learned that the complete removal of the breast was a completely different procedure than reducing them and required a surgeon who specialized in individuals who were transitioning.

His rationale made sense and I resigned to his choice. When Kamal reached out to the surgeon, he provided an over the phone consultation. I was leery of the lack of an initial physical examination; however, the surgeon assured us that he could provide a competent consultation and approve Kamal surgery using photos and blood work. Kamal could have the blood work done locally, and have the chosen lab send the results to the surgeon in Ohio. It was just that easy, but I was not too thrilled. Kamal, on the other hand, was elated to be one step closer to becoming the man he wanted to be.

It was all happening so fast and seemed surreal. The pending surgery, coupled with his much deeper voice and facial hair, made it all real. Ultimately, Kamal had his breasts removed and was out of commission for about a month. During his recovery, he had a great friend by the name of Goose who came and stayed the entire month to assist him in any way he needed. She did everything from making sure he took his meds to helping him bathe properly. Goose was a godsend, and I can't thank her enough. When Kamal fully healed, he returned to his life as scheduled. Not long afterward, my family and I relocated to North Carolina where Kamal now lives with his cat and dog. How he got those animals to get along is beyond me! Together, my family and I, take it day by day and thus far everything has been pretty awesome, to say the least.

In retrospect, I realize that Kamal made his own decisions during his period of transition and paid for his surgery with his own money. I have to admit that I take great pride in knowing that he made up his mind to do something, set his goals and followed through. It's an admirable quality and a mark of what type of person he is. It took some time, but I finally came to understand that despite any guilt I felt as a parent, I didn't do anything wrong when raising him. If there is one thing that remains true about Kamal, it's that the person he is has never changed. He still guides his life by the lessons I taught him while growing up. He still loves animals, hugs, and kisses. He still seeks advice from his mother, and he loves his brothers and sisters. With the exception of his outward appearance, he is the same person.

I raised all of my children, Kamal included, to be respectable human beings whose life goal should be to bring more to the world than they take. I raised them to have morals and to never look down on anyone. I instilled values in them. They are not, nor have ever been on drugs, never joined a gang, stayed out of trouble, and performed pretty well in school. I supported my transgender son, even when I did not fully understand all that was going. Outside of Kamal's struggles associated with coming to terms with his gender identity, and then his struggles with me because I had no idea what he was going through, I think I did a pretty good job as a parent. Particularly for a girl who was only 16 years old with two children. I did what I could with what I had, although it was not that much.

My children love me. I never abandoned them, and together we went through thick and thin as a family. We had our fair share of ups and downs, but in there were always more ups than downs, and for that I am grateful. As I became a more spiritual and grounded person, I realized that God took me through exactly what He wanted me to go through to become the person I am. My experiences with Kamal taught me to have an open mind and heart when it came to people and things I may not initially understand. I am thankful for the crazy and unpredictable journey I had with him because it afforded me the opportunity to meet a ton of wonderful people along the way. The best outcome of it all is the positive relationship Kamal and I now have.

AFTERWORD

The decision to share my life and journey with Kamal was not an easy one, by any stretch of the imagination. There were times when anger and frustration flooded back, and the pain of old wounds reappeared. It was as if I was reliving the moments all over again. I would often cry and have to take a break. Even then, I had to appreciate how far I have come from that naïve sixteen-year-old girl from Queens with two children attached to my hip and trying my best to escape an abusive relationship. It was not easy, but I made it. My advice to any parent who suffers from the scars of abuse, whether verbal or physical or who are having difficulty dealing with their children, both within and outside of the LGBTQ community, is to seek help! There is nothing to be ashamed of, and no reason to ever feel that you are broken or less than because you need counseling or therapy. Sometimes, talking to a professional who is removed from your situation is the best medicine. They will provide sound and honest feedback.

Additionally, counselors and therapists can recommend resources that may play a significant part in your healing or come in handy for you at some point in time. They may also be able to help remove you from your toxic situation, should it involve getting away from an abusive partner or spouse. If you are seeking aid of any kind, whether it is medical, housing or food assistance, I have always found that my counselor was always there to help. Do not feel like protecting yourself or your children is something to take lightly. I'll protect my children at all costs!

For children and young adults who feel like they can't talk to their parents, I urge you to speak to someone. Whether it be a guidance counselor at school, your doctor, a friend, an aunt or uncle, or your grandparents; please talk to someone. Keeping your feelings bottled up is not healthy, and can lead to unnecessary stress in your life. You may become agitated with others, develop a short temper or you may even lash out and strike people; but that is not the answer. You must talk to someone about what you are feeling. A simple conversation goes a long way. And if you have no one to talk to, please reach out to help lines that will allow you to vent over the phone and let go of whatever you are feeling. For your convenience, I have listed a few of these numbers in the back of this book.

Outside of all of that, there is nothing I can stress to parents more than loving your child unconditionally. Children need to know and feel they are loved; just like they need food to eat, water to drink, a roof over their heads and clothes on their backs. In fact, everyone needs love. We all want to feel accepted and supported. We all want to be able to say, without any doubt, that our family has our backs.

A LETTER TO KAMAL

The day you were born was one of the happiest days of my life. You were such a good baby. You woke up every four hours, on the dot, which allowed me to get some rest in between feedings. I remember how you would suck on your middle and your ring fingers. I always thought that it was odd for a baby to suck on those two particular fingers, but you refused the pacifier, so I allowed it. I had no idea that that innocent little face would bring me so many problems later on in life. I had no idea that my precious baby would give me a run for my money, but you did. I remember how you laughed at almost everything because it was just so funny to you. Your laughing would sometimes get you into trouble since you always laughed at the most inappropriate times. There were times you could not even control your laughter, and the only way I could get you to stop was to remind you that I was not playing around. I remember how at around the age of 8 years old, you began to like playing outside with Marquis and his friends; and concerned yourself more with what he was doing instead of worrying about yourself. If you got into trouble, you always brought Marquis into it, and I would have to tell you to worry about yourself! Although your bringing up Marquis would work my nerves, I thought it was cute that Marquis was always on your mind.

When you graduated from elementary school, I took you to get your hair done and bought a pretty white dress. Needless to say, you had a fit! You thought the dress was too dainty, and maybe even ugly, but you looked stunning to me. When I brought you to school that day, everybody thought you looked so beautiful! I now understand that I was trying to make you into what I wanted you to be; never realizing that I was forcing it down your throat. I remember the fights you had in junior high school and how you would start them for no apparent reason. But then call me to the school to bail you out of trouble. I remember seeing a change in you that I could not quite put my finger on, or maybe I was just in denial. Sometimes I thought the other children you hung around with were a bad influence on you, but with the knowledge that I have today, I can say that was not the case. You were probably struggling with what you were feeling, and not really knowing how to deal with it. Maybe even feeling like no one else felt the way you did.

When your teachers would call me, I would get so upset because I knew it was never good news. The only time a teacher would call me with good news was when you drew something spectacular, or one of your art projects was going to be featured at a gala. Thinking back at it now, I wonder if your energy and pent up frustration were why you played the piano so beautifully and drew so well at a young age. I knew back then you had a gift. I always thought you were creative, but I never knew you were struggling. Had I have known about the turmoil brewing inside of you; I promise you, I would've helped. I know that sometimes talking to me was not always easy, and maybe to this day it may still not be that easy, but I'm getting better at it. I really do try to listen and understand you before I speak to you. So, if I never said it to you then, I'll say it now, I'm sorry if I ever made you feel like you did not matter. I'm sorry if I ever made you feel like you could not come to me.

I hope my past mistakes with your father do not cause you any strife. Furthermore, I hope that you were never disgusted with me as your mother. I know I put you and Marquis through a lot. Trying to keep a family together that was never meant to be together was tough, but I'm sure it was tougher for you and Marquis because you were so young and did not have a choice. But I did it because at the time I thought it was what was best for you and your brother. You'll never have any idea of how much I love you until you become a parent one day, and you'll know everything I did, I did for my children.

Either way, this is a goodbye to the child that once was. You are not here anymore, and although I miss you at times, I have a wonderful second son. A son who bore with me when I could not remember his name; when I sometimes called him a "she" or a "her;" and who I sometimes have to remind that I am their mother and not their friend. I thank you for bearing with me as I learned there's no difference between the new you and the old you. And I thank you for knowing that I love you.

I pray that in life everything works out for you and in your favor. You're such a good kid and a dope individual. This world can be very evil and judgmental, and I pray that you never have to experience the type of evil I have experienced in this lifetime. I pray that your truth sets you free in more ways than one, and I pray that you live a happy and fruitful life. I pray that you ALWAYS know that Mommy loves you and that you can come to me with anything....except to co-sign stuff!

A PERSONAL NOTE

TO SOMEONE I WILL NOT NAME, BUT THANK YOU!

Thank you for exposing my family's truth! Thank you for putting me and my issues on blast for everyone to see. I struggled with some demons that I thought I could handle on my own, but I could not. If it were not for the pressure you placed on me, as well as my family; I do not think I would have ever faced my reality. If it were not for your hatred toward my child and me, there would not be love. If it were not for you telling my business to the world, I would've never had a much needed discussion with my child.

I was procrastinating, and you forced me to deal with what was in front of me. I chose to keep my personal business private only because I was worried about what the world would think. But thanks to you, I am a proud mom who is not ashamed of what goes on in my life, and I flaunt my love for my children aloud and in public. I could not care less what people think about my family or me because we live in LOVE! We follow the path of Allah and nothing is greater than that! People will judge, just like you did, but it does not affect me anymore.

I have grown, and I have to thank you for that. I have grown into a woman that does not get so upset when someone talks behind my back. I rather talk things out instead of going toe to toe or blow for blow with someone. I do not keep bad company around me or befriend individuals that give me a bad vibe. I know within seconds of meeting someone if that person is bad news, and so I stay away instead of thinking *it's just me.* I do not look to befriend anyone in this industry we call "Entertainment." I either genuinely like you or I don't. My family is as tight as we'll ever be, there are no secrets, and it's all because of YOU!

I am grateful to have had you in my life. Even if it was just for a brief moment, you taught me some very valuable lessons. And immediately after you taught me those lessons, you were completely out of my life. So for these reasons, I thank you. I thank you because I have learned from you. I have learned how to choose my friends, how to value my family, how to treat people, and to deal with my issues head on instead of thinking they would somehow magically disappear. You have made me stronger, and because of you, I value my REAL friends because Lord knows friends do not come easy. I pray you are doing well, and that God continues to bless you because I have no ill will towards you. I used to, but not anymore. Allah has eased my soul and all things negative has flowed out. I do not have the energy for negativity anymore; it is thoroughly draining. I am all about peace, love, and prosperity. I hope you are doing the same.

So to all of those out there who are fighting their own battles and inner demons, I pray for you with love.

-Viv

Vivian Billings, also known as 'Gossip Viv' was first introduced to the entertainment industry in 2001 working as the talent coordinator for "All Access DVD," a then very popular media outlet. Soon after, Billings began penning her experiences while on set, gathering the inside scoop or "gossip" on some of the industry's most popular personalities. The lives of our favorite celebrities are always in the spotlight and someone needed to report it, and in the most accurate way. Vivian decided that she would launch her own website and become the insider who brought the information to the masses.

Established in 2008, Vivian launched HipHopGossipSite.com as a platform to provide the online audience with the latest news and 'gossip' about everyone's favorite celebrities, along with exclusive content including photos, videos, new music and more. Gaining much notoriety from the popular site, coupled with her infectious personality, Vivian went on to work alongside Lisa Evers of *Hot 97 Street Soldiers*, *The Star & Buc Wild Show* and Urban Latino Radio.

With all of her gossip blogs and radio segments, Vivian then caught the attention of VH1 executives who were looking for a fresh face to add to their new reality docu-series show titled *The Gossip Game*. Alongside the likes of Angela Yee of Power 105.1's *The Breakfast Club* and Kim Osorio of "The Source Magazine," Vivian was added to the roster of the new show.

After a few years of conducting interviews, Vivian and her family relocated to Charlotte, North Carolina where you can occasionally catch her on Power 98 FM reporting the latest news and gossip on *The Morning Madhouse* alongside No Limit Larry and Burpie. Vivian is still an integral member of the G-Unit/ThisIs50.com team and travels frequently to New York where she interviews celebrities, and asks them all of the juicy questions to keep her audience entertained.

If you or someone you know would like to support an organization that provides the Trans Community with the tools needed to achieve their personal goals please donate to Community Kinship Life (CK Life) at **www.cklife.org.**

Kamal, 2017

If you or someone you know is transgender or struggling with their gender identity and is experiencing a crisis, please contact the Trans Lifeline at
US: (877) 565-8860 Canada: (877) 330-6366
or visit their website at **www.translifeline.org.**

If you or someone you know is lesbian, gay, bisexual, transgender or queer and in need of assistance, please contact the
LGBT National Hotline at **(888) 843-4564**
or visit their website at **www.glbthotline.org.**

If you or someone you know is a victim of domestic violence, please contact the
National Domestic Violence Hotline at (800) **799-7233**
or visit their website at **www.thehotline.org.**

NOV 2 9 2017

CPSIA information can be obtained
at www.ICGtesting.com
Printed in the USA
LVOW11s0107281017
554097LV00001B/35/P

9 780692 806272